Also by Wendy Crisp Lestina

From the Back Pew
Old Favorites from Ferndale Kitchens

And, writing as Wendy Reid Crisp,

100 Things I'm Not Going To Do Now That I'm Over 50
Do As I Say, Not As I Did
When I Grow Up, I Want To Be 60

A BIT OF EARTH

A BIT OF EARTH

Distributed by Partners West
Bellingham, Washington

ISBN 13: 978-0-9882887-6-8
ISBN 10: 0-9882887-6-1
Library of Congress Control Number: 2015955098

Grateful acknowledgement is made to the *Ferndale Enterprise*, in which most of these pieces first appeared as weekly columns. They have been revised for inclusion in this book.

LYCHGATE PRESS
editor@lychgatepress. com
www. lychgatepress. com

Cover design by Terry Lim Graphic Design
Cover photos by George Waldner, Anderson Studio, and Caroline Titus

In memory of Helaine Shilling
whose love and grace glow
in the family she left too soon

CONTENTS

PREFACE

"Is there anything you want…Do you want toys, books dolls?"
"Might I," quavered Mary, "might I have a bit of earth?"

Frances Hodgson Burnett
The Secret Garden
1911

I was 49 when I inherited my bit of earth, the farm of George and Hazel Waldner, my aunt and uncle. The bit is a generous morsel: 80 acres of pastures and Sitka spruce-covered hills, a half-mile from the Pacific Ocean at the northern end of California's Lost Coast.

The spoiler in paradise is geology. The farm is located about forty miles due east of the off-shore Triple Junction. There, two massive tectonic plates, the North American and the Pacific, lurch in a sideslip against each other as a third plate, the aggressive little Gorda, attempts to jam itself under them in a potentially cataclysmic configuration called the Cascadia Subduction Zone.

I think about this once or twice a day.

The first time I lived in the Waldner farmhouse, I was four. George had returned from World War II, which he spent in Los Angeles publishing a newspaper for an Army battalion, to a family that had doubled in size. No longer a childless couple, Hazel and George now sheltered my widowed mother and me. They bought Paolo Gabrielli's abandoned dairy farm for $10,000, and tore down the barn, the chicken house, and the outhouse, and built a new house that exactly replicated the house Paolo had built, a house that had exactly replicated the house he had left in Italy in the pre-Great War months of 1914. Carefully preserved by Hazel and George, however, was the grapevine, a summer curtain over the porch grown from slips Paolo had sewn inside the lining of his coat jacket when he emigrated.

Shortly after we moved into the new house, my mother enrolled me in Sunday school, where I was told to memorize the 23rd Psalm. The Song of David made perfect sense to me. Green pastures and still waters were outside the wide dining room windows in the new house, and if the long afternoon shadows were intimations of death, I feared no evil. How could I? Three sweet-faced elderly ladies watched over me, doting and protective.

I was well into adulthood when, during a pastoral reading of the 23rd Psalm at a funeral service, I suddenly listened to the words as the vision of the loving women appeared. I wish I hadn't. I wish I'd continued moving through life in the unquestioning, comforting company of Shirley and her friends, Goodness and Mercy.

A Bit of Earth began as a compilation of a few of the newspaper columns I've written over the past 15 years for the *Ferndale Enterprise*. Slowly, the necessary editing became rewriting, and then, retelling. The stories are as true as human memory permits—but some of the names are not; I changed them when I knew someone would appreciate obscurity in stories told from my point of view.

When I moved back to Waldner Farm, I thought I had made all my mistakes off-stage. I believed a life of peace stretched before me. Soon after I arrived, I wrote that the world was "vast and green and forever." I was confident I understood life, and I was ready to share my unique wisdom. I wrote two books, saying as much. They were very short books.

This one is longer.

Wendy Crisp Lestina
September 2016

JOHNNY AT THE RIVER

My father visited me once, in a dream when I was 50. In the dream I was standing on the river bar, barefooted. It was August in far-northern California and the slow, sullen Eel River was threaded with thick strands of algae. The flow of water had receded since the winter and the rounded stones of the dry bed were exposed, dusty, and hot as city sidewalks.

He came up behind me, on my right. I didn't turn. I knew who it was and I knew he was wearing shoes, street shoes, on the river bar.

The soles of my feet burned. I wanted to move, to walk over the uneven cobbling into the water's shallow edge and balance on the slimy rocks amid the tadpoles and minnows.

I sensed he was a small man.

In the wedding photographs, my father is slighter than my mother and a breath or two shorter—she was five-foot-eight before she was ancient—and his face is narrower, his features more delicate.

"I want to come home." He spoke simply, in a voice that had been trained to give orders with the assurance they would be followed.

"Tell them I want to get out of there. Have them dig up the bones and burn them. I want my ashes sprinkled in the river on the opening day of trout season."

Then he was gone, without telling me he loved me and before I could tell him that the river is not as he remembers. Dams now divert its waters to southern vineyards. Only for a few weeks in the winter do the silver, muscular fish run, when rains replenish the diversion, when they have some place to run to.

And he wants to come home? What is he talking about? He visited Humboldt County exactly once, on his honeymoon. He never fished here. The closest he got to the Eel River was sitting on a rock on the beach of a small resort in the redwoods. ("Wild huckleberry pie!" he wrote, in white ink, on the black pages of a photo album that he gave to my mother to memorialize the first week of their marriage.)

Dutifully, I wrote to the Golden Gate National Cemetery in San Bruno, south of San Francisco, and asked about the procedure for disinterring a body from the rows of white crosses.

The director responded promptly, advising me that this was rarely done, and that it was a gesture not regarded with great favor. Further—and this was the deal breaker—my situation was more complicated than most. The director explained that my paternal grandparents, John Domer Robertson, Sr., and his wife, Ethel, had been permitted to be buried in the same plot on top of their son, Johnny.

If Johnny was disinterred, I was told, all three Robertsons would be removed from the cemetery. I asked why. John, Sr. was an Army veteran who served under John Pershing in 1916 on the Mexican border in a fruitless hunt for Pancho Villa and in 1918 at the Battle of Verdun on the Western Front.

My question was not answered.

The cost to me, the director said, would be at least $5,000.

That conversation took place over 20 years ago. I've visited the gravesite several times in the interval, and it is unsettling, knowing that three key members of my family are crammed into a single small plot as though they were alive and helpless, and sharing a one-room tenement.

I've done nothing to liberate Johnny. I've settled for the decision that, unless he is able to muster enough energy for another spiritual visitation, I probably never will.

It's not as if I haven't already let him down. In another ghostly encounter, I might have to answer to him for the loss of his Silver Star.

It happened in August, 1980. I was living in northern Westchester County, New York. I was divorced and the mother of a four-year-old son, Max, who was spending the month in Ferndale with my mother, Maxine, and Doc, the veterinarian she married when I was five years old. (When I was seven, Doc legally adopted me and I took his surname. I referred to him as my dad. He referred to me as his stepdaughter.)

The freedom from parental responsibility granted by Max's summer in Ferndale gave me the opportunity to sublet a loft in Manhattan near Lafayette and Spring streets, with Robert, an attorney I was dating.

Those 31 days of that August are the sum total of my thirty-something adventures in New York.

Robert and I spent evenings sitting on the fire escape, eight or ten floors below the skyline of water towers and rooftop gardens. After midnight, we'd join his friends in the Bowery and go to CBGB, a bar that featured punk rock bands. We'd smoke cigarettes and drink beer until the 4 a.m. closing. Often, that wasn't the end of the party—a few blocks away, there was an after-hours blues joint where we could welcome the dawn.

Days, I rode uptown on the Lexington subway to my job as an editor of *Datamation*, a computer trade journal.

The workday started at 9 a.m. I was never notably late, nor did I take naps at my desk. I was in New York, working on Fifth Avenue, living in Soho. I had money, free time, friends, and warm nights. I was never tired.

Sometimes when friends say optimistic, cheerful remarks about themselves, such as "I may look 70, but I feel 35," I recall that summer when I *was* 35, and how I felt: exhilarated. I breathed only the charged essence of freedom.

On the last day of August, Robert and I packed up the few belongings we'd brought to the loft and shoved them into his car, which may have been a '73 bronze Mercury Capri hatchback. We drove uptown to 104th and Broadway, where Robert's twin brother Gordon shared a flat with three fellow alumni from Lawrence University.

The sublet in Soho had been furnished. All I'd packed from my house in Pound Ridge were necessities—clothes, cosmetics, and sentimental items I was reluctant to leave in an unoccupied house in the woods. Most special was the Silver Star that had been awarded to my father for losing his life while saving the lives of two of his men in the 6th Marines, Company K, on Okinawa in 1945.

The ceremony for the posthumous award was held nearly three years after his death. I was selected by the family to be the physical recipient, a compromise my mother made with John Sr. and Ethel, who believed it should reside with them.

To receive the award, my mother and I traveled the 225 miles from Ferndale to the Alameda Naval Air Station on the east side of San Francisco Bay. Many photographs were taken, mostly of me, a solemn-eyed four-year-old, gazing up at the officiating naval commander as he knelt to pin the beribboned star on the smocking of my starched dress. I don't remember any of it.

The medal was in my possession from that moment until the morning of September 1, 1980. Robert and I went downstairs to the car to find the windows of the Merc smashed and all our stuff gone, including the box of Johnny's campaign ribbons and marksmanship medals, two Purple Hearts, and the Silver Star.

I'd partied, I'd played, I'd paid a high price.

4

Two years passed. In the fall of 1982, long after Robert and I were no longer dating, he called and asked if he could drop by for a visit.

"I have something for you," he said.

He arrived with a manila folder of letters from various Pentagon officials. The papers documented Robert's lengthy and ultimately successful efforts to have my father's decorations and awards replaced. Robert handed me the two Purple Hearts, the Silver Star, and a proclamation from the Secretary of the Navy, James V. Forrestal, which Robert read aloud.

"I read this to my mother when it came in the mail," Robert said. "We both cried."

Rita, Robert's mother, was English. As a young woman she had lived in London during the blitz. The night I met her, she was sitting in her drawing room drinking a gin and tonic and watching the news. The Irish Republican Army had just blown up a pleasure boat on which Louis Francis Albert Victor Nicholas, 1st Earl Mountbatten of Burma, Admiral of the Fleet, had been a passenger.

"They've killed Dickie!" Rita cried.

The new medals, the replacements, were rarely seen after Robert's visit. The next day, I drove to a bank in Armonk, and rented a safe deposit box in which to store them. As the years passed and I have moved back and forth and up and down throughout the country, these artifacts of war have retained the highest level of security, moving with me at full attention from vault to vault.

I never saw my father, unless I count his visit on the river bar—and how can I? I didn't even turn around.

John Domer Robertson, Jr., graduated from the University of California's law school, Boalt Hall, in 1942, and within four months had passed the California bar exam, enlisted in the U.S. Marines, and married Maxine Folendorf, whom his parents called "that German nurse."

In July, 1943, when Maxine was two months pregnant, Johnny shipped out of San Diego to the South Pacific.

Twenty-two months and five amphibious landings later, he was killed by a Japanese sniper. That is the central story of my life, and of Johnny's, and he has never let me forget it.

THE FEAR-LACED FIFTIES

At a Halloween party, I had staked out a spot at the end of the buffet table and was ravaging the cheese when the conversation meandered to high school.

"Your sister," said Pete Bansen, the host, referring to Tonya, "was in the 'Mighty Crew of '72.' Our motto was 'Great Are We of '73.' Four years later, the motto was 'Thank Heaven for '77.'"

The discussion put me in a funk.

A class motto. Just one more cool thing, like girls being able to play interscholastic sports, that we didn't have at Ferndale High in the pre-pill, pre-Vatican II, pre-Title-IX, pre-rock-and-roll era.

I belong to the tiniest generation of the 20th Century, the cohort born between the two Sundays that encompassed the 1,346 days from December 7, 1941, to August 15, 1945.

Not Depression kids, not baby boomers. We are war babies and we were born into circumstances that demanded our beautiful mothers abandon the delights of their brief romances and accept with grace what was hoped to be a temporary displacement. The war defined us, even if some of us had fathers who didn't go to war, who were too old or who worked in essential industries or who failed the medical examination.

There was no honor in safety. Men who didn't serve in the armed forces during World War II, regardless of what scientific, social or material benefits they contributed, spent their lifetimes shadowed by the fear of irrelevance.

This is not a theory. When Doc was 18, he rode the bus to San Francisco with his brother and their cousins to enlist in the U.S. Navy. The selective service doctors detected a heart murmur and sent Doc home, dismissed with a classification of 4F—"unfit for service."

Doc went to college and on to veterinary school. His brother went to the South Pacific, his cousins to Europe and Alaska, and his high school friends to every theater of the war. Several were killed and the rest served out their days in various degrees of undiagnosed battle fatigue.

Doc never believed he accomplished enough to make up for his failure to be fit for military service, and he was haunted by the hero who had preceded him as his wife's first husband. Until the last few years of his life, Doc was uncomfortable with me, never assuming the role of father, forever deferring to my mother and my aunt as though he had no rights, despite legal and financial evidence to the contrary.

Study the context, history professors tell us. No individual, however young, however geographically remote, lives outside the crucible of world events.

As children, my friends and I had fun riding bicycles, roller skating, playing board games, roaring an outboard up Salt River, chasing the little kids down the alleys. Always, there was an underscore of *gravitas.*

I studied the context. The first day of school for the children who were to be the high school graduating class of 1961 was August 29, 1949. In the Eel River Valley, we walked into first grade at one of the six rural schools or the town school or the Catholic school just a few hours after the Soviet Union had successfully exploded its first atomic bomb.

On the second day of school, we went to our desks, looked up at the Parker penmanship alphabet strung across the blackboard, and were told then or later, if not by our teachers or our parents, by each other—someone knew the score—that any minute the Russians might bomb us and we might die.

Although it would be several years before civil defense videos featured a cartoon turtle that showed us how to "duck and cover" to avoid nuclear death, we became perpetually anxious, fascinated and terrified by our own stories that were constructed from fragments of what we overheard on the radio, what the grownups said, and what we glimpsed in newsstand comic books.

A fragment from a sunny afternoon in the spring of 1952: I'm walking along Ocean Avenue to Fifth Street in Ferndale. I lived in town now, having left the ranch six months after my mother and Doc returned from their honeymoon. (It took that long, ostensibly, for a carpenter to finish remodeling my bedroom. By the time I was invited to join the family, my mother was four months' pregnant with my sister Candace.)

On this particular afternoon, I wasn't thinking about my family. I was in the second grade. I was thinking about the cobalt bomb.

Cobalt Blue was a color in Binney & Smith's Crayola line, a medium icy blue slightly tinged with green. I understood the bomb to be a massive blue balloon that spewed poisonous fire as it floated over the top of the elementary school.

What was the cobalt bomb? I looked it up. A cobalt bomb is a "salted bomb," a nuclear weapon designed to produce enhanced amounts of radioactive fallout.

"The concept of a cobalt bomb was originally described in a radio program by physicist Leo Szilard on February 26, 1950," the Wikipedia entry reads. That would have been the day the class celebrated Janet Crane's sixth birthday. Her mother would have brought cupcakes and Kool-Aid to school.

"Szilard suggested that an arsenal of cobalt bombs would be capable of destroying all human life on Earth," Wikipedia adds, reassuring us that "his conclusions are disputed." In any case, "as far as is publicly known, no cobalt bombs have ever been built."

That was news to me. As I child, I did not understand the cobalt bomb was theoretical. What I did know was that there was a bomb even worse than the rest and the Communists were going to drop it on us because we believed in God and because Americans could say anything out loud that they wanted to say unless they were children or girls. ("Keep your big mouth shut," my mother said frequently.)

The Russians were coming to America after the bomb was dropped (and, presumably, after the fallout had dispersed) and they were coming not as soldiers, but—as portrayed in the government-produced movies we were forced to watch when it rained at recess—as white men in black suits and black ties and fedoras. (The Communists closely resembled the men in the other movies who drove black cars and offered bags of candy to potential kidnap victims.)

The state films were narrated by stentorian male voices, Voices of Authority.

We could be hurt, we were by the V of A, "in different ways," if we weren't ready for "such a big explosion, it can smash in buildings..." and throw us "against trees and walls." The atomic bomb flash "could burn you worse than a terrible sunburn."

Class motto? How about "'61? We're done."

It was never clear, in those fear-laced '50s, what would deliver our deaths: the bomb, the Russians or the mutants. We went to the Hart Theater and watched a movie about irradiated ants, *The Mole People, The Beast from 20,000 Fathoms, Tarantula,* and *Creature From the Black Lagoon.* (The latter was my favorite because during the scary parts Gerald Kukuk held my hand, a sweet remedy for thermonuclear terror.)

If, in our early teens, we doubted the reality of this hysteria, our adolescent optimism took a blow three weeks into our freshman year when, on October 4, 1957, the radio news of the Soviet Union's successful launch of Sputnik was played over Ferndale Union High School's public address system. Now, even if there were mudslides on Highway 101, the Russians could reach Humboldt County.

We got religion. That day after school and all days thereafter, a clump of us, boys and girls, claimed our territory at Martin's Soda Fountain and sat for 90 minutes—until it was time to help mothers cook or fathers milk cows—and we argued about God, the infallibility of the Pope (the notoriously fallible Pius XII), the existence of purgatory, the second coming, the nature of sin as it related directly to our lives, particularly in the form of whatever it was we were doing with each other while parked in dark country lanes, and, mostly, the afterlife: specifically, who would be there and who would not.

Ferndale had six churches.

I went to the Congregational because that's where my friends went. Doc, who'd been raised in the Danish Lutheran church, never attended once in my memory. George was a Christian Scientist who read Mary Baker Eddy at home. Hazel was a Methodist, part of the first batch of siblings, the "South Dakota five," whose childhoods were steeped in the affluence their father, my grandfather, provided via his hardware store. (Methodism, a branch of Anglicanism, is a purely American denomination, which means its people are always moving farther west. Once a Methodist hits the Pacific coast, the church has pretty much done its job.)

My mother was one of the "California three" siblings doomed to be born at the poor end of my grandparents' economic cycle and raised under the single promise my grandmother elicited in exchange for her willingness to move west: that all future children would be Baptists.

There wasn't a Baptist church in Ferndale. My mother, unable to find a congregation in which she was comfortable, fantasized about attending church. On more than one

Mother's Day, she spent the day in bed with the shades drawn. "All I asked for is for the whole family to attend church together," she said, refusing our cold French toast.

Being a Baptist without a church wasn't easy. She loved to dance and play cards—forbidden treats she rarely bypassed—she was and is a cauldron of dogmatic confusion. "That German nurse" worked in emergency rooms in Oakland hospitals in the late 1930s and early 1940s, and there, her experiences shaped her as a medical feminist. She was unwavering in opinions about rape victims (male and female), back-street abortions, and pregnancy-forced marriages. Lifelong and to this day (she is 102 and well as of this writing), she has been a fierce ally in her daughters' rights to choose. And yet, without displaying an ironic drop of self-awareness, she is simultaneously a pious, evangelical pro-lifer whose closest friends are Biblical conservatives.

The voices around the Formica-and-chrome tables at Martin's repeated lessons learned in Catholic catechism and in Lutheran confirmation classes, doctrine read in the Episcopal *Book of Common Prayer* and heard in Pentecostal sermons. For a class that was to cross the graduation line as 52 individuals, we spanned the Christian spectrum with impressive breadth. There were no atheists; our obsession with eschatology was not intellectual. We needed to believe we would survive.

We did have a class motto, of sorts. It was "1961: the first upside-down year since 1881 and the last until 6009." And therein hangs the war babies' bid for exceptionalism.

OVERDUE

At its monthly meeting in February 2012, the board of directors of the Ferndale Library voted favorably on an issue that was included on its agenda at my request. A day or so later, I received a letter from the president.

"The Ferndale Library Board is pleased to inform you of its decision and the following motion...After discussion regarding the request of Wendy Lestina for reinstatement of night-time privileges, unaccompanied by an adult...privileges are hereby reinstated...suspending the requirement for accompaniment by an adult."

A year earlier, the Ferndale Library, built with funds donated by the industrial philanthropist Andrew Carnegie, had commemorated its centennial with a gala celebration in song, verse, and oratory.

One of the opening speakers was the mayor, Jeff Farley, who was also a member of the library's board of directors.

"The library was a big part of our lives when we were growing up," Jeff proclaimed. "We studied here, played cards in here..."

He said more. I didn't hear it. *We played cards in here?!* And now he's on the *library board?* He was ten years behind me in school, coming of age in a decade when—evidently—the old rules were replaced with no rules.

In 1959, when I was 15, I was forbidden to go to the library during its evening hours unless my mother ("an adult") went with me. I had been banned without a hearing, punished for playing poker with a group of boys.

Jeff's off-hand remark led me to my request to the library board for reinstatement. I was, after all, approaching an age when there would be no adult older than I.

The first two times I mentioned it to Bonnie, the head librarian, she chuckled. The third time she said, "Wendy, are you serious about this?"

I said I was.

I had written about my expulsion once or twice before in a newspaper column. I anticipated that after its publication, I would be swiftly forgiven, maybe even receive a 50-years-overdue apology. I didn't. People said they loved the column.

"What a hoot," said my friend Mary Ellen. "You were quite a troublemaker."

Mary Ellen's father had died a few months before she was born, and her brother, sixteen years her elder, was a Marine at the battle of Guadalcanal, and the first Ferndale boy killed in World War II. Her mother did not remarry in a candlelight wedding and begin a new family; her mother and a clutch of aunts and cousins hovered over her and thus Mary Ellen had not been allowed to frequent adolescent gathering places like Martin's Soda Fountain and the Thursday-night library poker games.

In 1959 my family numbered five: my mother, Doc, nine-year-old Candace, and five-year-old Tonya. We had moved from the tiny Fifth Street house to a two-story 1917 craftsman built on a lot adjacent to the Ferndale Public Library. From the east-facing upstairs bedroom window, I could peer directly through the library's back window that had an unimpeded view of the library's windowed front door.

We moved to the big house when I was in the fourth grade. I was already a compulsive reader, in trouble with my mother every day for having my "nose in a book" rather than doing my chores. Now I could read without being caught. I could hide among the stacks and go anywhere, be anyone. On the library shelves were throngs of children whose lives, tumbling off the pages, were as mine, confusing and contradictory. Their dangers, however, were tangible. They were chased by evil trolls, they survived fires and floods, their dogs ran away, their horses were killed. Bad people stole them, good people died. Very often, the children who lived on the shelves had no parents, or at most, one parent who was—luckily for them—preoccupied with the vagaries of adult life.

My friends and I read constantly, racing through the Oz books, the Mother West Wind Stories, Raggedy Ann, the Bobbsey twin series, the endless Nancy Drews. We progressed from the bottom shelves up, and as we grew taller, the subjects became more complex. I devoured the nonfiction of John Gunther, Sue read all of Rex Stout, Janet was absorbed in the novels of Daphne DuMaurier. If Hazel Flowers, the head librarian, wasn't there to censor our choices, there were no limits.

The library had evening hours on Thursdays. Most parents were relieved to watch their teenagers leave the house with homework, headed for a quiet, public place. For town kids, the anticipation of Thursday night was charged with excitement.

"Town kids" was a label that did not include all the children who lived in town. It was a euphemism, a catch-call for the random offspring of the broken, widowed, divorced, blended families who were not woven into the religious and ethnic networks. We had no old-country traditions to celebrate or scorn, no consistent parental rules. Unlike the "country kids," the catch-all for everyone else, we were not related to other families in the valley. We were our own nomadic clan, and the library was one of our oases.

On Thursday nights, shortly before the seven o'clock opening, I would enter Candace's east-facing upstairs bedroom, void whatever rights she feebly attempted to assert, and settle in by the window.

Soon, through the series of aligned windows, the boys could be seen entering the library alone or in pairs. I ran downstairs, out the kitchen door, and joined them.

The "gang," a word the library board was to use against us, included some combination of five or six boys 14-16 years old, occasionally one or two of their sisters, and me.

Initially, we had good intentions—to do homework. That noble goal faltered and we began playing nickel-ante five-card draw. We talked and laughed in a strained, quasi-quiet mode. There were guffaws. Someone got bonked on the head with an algebra book.

The night librarian, Mrs. Broner, who was deaf, patrolled the stacks to our enclave—a strong square table with six chairs huddled against the complete works of Zane Grey—and shook her index finger at us.

Before the school year ended, the library's board of directors reviewed the situation as reported to them by Mrs. Broner and "several citizens." A gang of juvenile delinquents had taken over the library. Townspeople were "uncomfortable" and "nervous" about coming to the library at night. Edith Broner was threatening to resign. Something had to be done.

I was expelled.

Mrs. Broner—and evidently "several citizens"—didn't know any of the boys or their sisters. I was the only child everyone recognized.

At home, I received no additional discipline.

In the past few years, reviewing the episode and unable to recall my parents' response to the public shaming, I became curious and called my mother.

"I remember the whole thing quite plainly," she said. "They called you a juvenile delinquent. I wasn't upset with you. I was upset with everybody else. I was very angry with Hazel Flowers, with all of them."

I was stunned by the uncharacteristic immediacy and forcefulness of her response. She had been on my side! And she had been right. The reaction of the library board was excessive, and its questionable justice was meted out unfairly.

On behalf of the adolescent I was, I am grateful the current board has reinstated me.

And to my mother, *brava*.

The statute of limitations on revelations of parental loyalty and honor never expires.

DOWN BELOW

In mid-August 1965, Dan and I drove a U-Haul trailer from Walla Walla, Washington, to Los Angeles. I was 21. Dan was 22. We'd been married a year.

Two months earlier, we'd graduated from college with degrees in English (me) and economics (Dan). We moved to Los Angeles because Dan, despite the cloud of fear over his 1-A military classification during the buildup in Vietnam and his choice of a non-essential field of study, had enrolled in the University of Southern California's Graduate School of Business.

My job was to find a job.

When we passed Carmel, I entered new latitudes. The farthest south I'd traveled from Ferndale was Pebble Beach, slightly north of Carmel, where Dan's grandmother lived. That magical enclave was an exception to the belief with which I'd been raised—that all points south of San Francisco, the "City," were "down below," a progressive disintegration of landscape and humanity that stretched to the nadir of civilization, Los Angeles.

Driving into L.A. on Highway 101, we were welcomed by random, skinny palm trees that rose like used toothbrushes among squat, faded, dusty houses.

Dan guided his white convertible through detoured traffic. We were waved passed police barriers to our destination, the corner of Vermont and Exposition, where USC had erected its married students' housing.

The building would have lost a design competition with similar structures in the Soviet Union. I have since visited prisons with more *feng shui.*

We had been assigned a studio apartment on the 14th floor. Two narrow day beds doubled as living room furniture that could be pulled out at right angles at bedtime—but not before the ironing board had been refolded into a nearby wall. The eating space was a ledge that hung off the back of the stove. When hoisted up, it had enough space for four plates, side by side, all eyes forward into the narrow kitchen with 20-foot ceilings (in land-scarce Los Angeles, it was efficient to meet square-foot requirements by building up, even if it meant—and it did—cabinets beyond even the reach of six-foot Dan's extended arms).

We couldn't sleep in the same bed together and we couldn't sit across a table and talk to each other.

A row of tall, severe windows with navy-blue, accordion-pleated motel draperies overlooked South Vermont Avenue, a street with USC on one side and rows of small businesses—appliance stores, drug stores, barbershops, grocers, wig shops—on the other.

I opened some of the boxes Dan had carried up from the U-Haul.

Out the window was the blazing inferno of our neighborhood. Throngs of people were smashing store windows along South Vermont to the accompaniment of a constant staccato of gunfire coming from the roofs of nearby university buildings. I could see the snipers, moving figures against the horizon I assumed were police.

Up to that evening, I'd heard gunshots only during duck hunting season.

The marauders were black people—we had just begun to use that word as a replacement for "colored," the appellation we had been taught was respectful. We were committed to respect and we were committed to civil rights.

A year earlier, as an act of unity with the Freedom Summer activists in the South, Dan and I had marched the streets of Walla Walla behind a pale Presbyterian minister. Weeks before, Dan and his fraternity brothers had boycotted a barber who had refused to cut the hair of an exchange student from Malawi, one of two black students on campus.

Outside the window overlooking South Vermont Avenue in Los Angeles, men and boys carried console television sets

"They're stealing!" I shouted to Dan, who was standing next to me smoking a Tareyton.

The air was shredded by sirens.

This vision of purgatory was frightening but not surprising. The looting hordes, the burning cars, the chaos of urban warfare, all were within the dramatic parameters of my anxious imagination. I was "down below."

I cried that my life was over. Dan said that it probably wasn't.

Early the next morning, we returned the U-Haul and, against his parents' gracefully expressed concerns, we drove away on our postponed honeymoon to Mexico.

Two weeks later, on a side table in the lobby of our hotel in Mazatlán, I spotted a copy of the classified ad section of a fairly recent Sunday *Los Angeles Times.*

Help Wanted, Women. As an English major who had rejected acquiring a teaching credential ("You won't have anything to fall back on!" my mother cried over the telephone when I told her I'd dropped Elementary Education. "What would have happened to us if I hadn't been a nurse?!"), my options were limited to one category: secretary.

I'd already had years of experience with secretarial work because I'd begun an after-school job at the *Ferndale Enterprise* when I was in the fifth grade—my uncle George was the publisher—and I'd never stopped working part-time in offices. I hadn't taken shorthand in high school; I had, however, developed an effective ersatz version to take notes in college. I'd owned an electric typewriter—a blue Smith-

21

Corona portable in a brown leather case—since my eleventh birthday.

I had little interest, however, in being simply a secretary. I wanted to be a Girl Friday. I'd seen Girl Fridays in movies. They were tall, smart, auburn-haired women in pencil skirts and tailored white silk blouses, very much like Aunt Fritzi in the *Nancy and Sluggo* comic books.

I spread the advertising section of the *Times* on our bed, and ran my finger down the Secretary/Girl Friday listings, stopping at one.

"Girl Friday. National trade magazine. 75 wpm, good telephone skills. College degree req. Must be bright, energetic, and cheerful."

It was a message in a bottle, a communication meant only for me.

We had two more weeks of honeymooning. The job would be gone before we got back to L.A. I went to the front desk at the hotel. A tropical storm had struck, and the wind was whipping through the lobby.

"I need some writing paper," I said. "Please. And if I could borrow your typewriter?"

I was given several sheets of thin blue stationery, the kind associated with airmail letters. At the top was a seagull in flight over the words Hotel Playa Mazatlán.

The typewriter's ribbon cylinders were missing, and a four-inch piece of black-and-red ribbon that fit directly in the clasp where the keys hit had to be held in place by whatever hand wasn't typing.

"Why isn't this resume in correct form?" I wrote at the top. I said where I was and who I was and how, even though I was only 21, I had twelve years of work experience.

I addressed an envelope with a matching seagull, stamped it, put it in a mailbox by the front door of the hotel, and thus launched a trial balloon into the skies of the real world.

On the way home, traveling north on Highway 15, somewhere south of Guaymas, Dan and I picked up a young hitchhiker, who told us about his good life.

22

"I have a smiling wife with rosy cheeks," he said, "I have a house. A garden. A cow."

I was dismayed by his optimism, by the idea of a life that held little more than a house, a garden, and a cow.

Especially the cow part. I was only four years out of Ferndale and I'd had my fill of cows. The big house on its five acres included a barn, two calf sheds, and a chicken house. Doc kept a half-dozen registered Guernseys in the fields and milked them twice a day, before and after work.

My mother and I never went out to the barn; still, we couldn't avoid the cows. The veterinary office closed at 5:00 p.m. My mother and the wife of my father's partner alternated weeks of being "on call."

There was no private telephone number in our house. We two families were on a three-party line with the office. When the telephone rang and we were on call, my mother or I would answer.

"Doctor Detlefsen's."

"Is Doc in?"

"No, he's not here right now. May I take a message?"

Whether Doc was home or not, this was the required response because we had to perform triage. Some ailments were emergencies; some could wait until the next day. Unless an animal was rabid, cows had priority—they were the valley's primary economic unit. By the same formula, tiny indoor dogs ranked last.

Emergencies were bloat, milk fever, "can't calf," and "cow down."

My mother or I would listen to the farmer or his wife describe the problem while we wrote the particulars in a lined spiral notebook that Marie, the office manager, would later use for billing.

Wednesday, April 3. Walter Pohler. Milk fever.

Answering the telephone when we were on call was intimidating, even when I was in high school. The farmers weren't reassured when they heard a kid's voice, and often, they were embarrassed to tell a young woman exactly what the medical issue was. Further, many of the older dairymen were from the "old country"—the Azores, Swiss villages, small farms in northern Italy or Denmark—and their English was limited.

June 4. Riverside Joe Mendes. Bloat.

Often, I would answer the phone, say that Doc was out, and the dairyman would say, "Is your mother home?" Everyone was comfortable with my mother. Not only was she friendly, she'd worked in the town's medical office for four years, and she'd had far more intimate conversations with these families than whether or not Daisy had a sore tit.

As soon as I moved away from Ferndale, I cashed in on the cows.

During matriculation week at Whitman, freshman women were invited to the house of a married couple who were on the faculty. Both had PhDs: he in math, she in astronomy.

"We're a paradox!" she told us. I thought that was the cleverest pun I'd ever heard.

At the freshman tea we sat in a circle and played an ice-breaker game in which we had to share something about ourselves, something that we had done that we thought no one else present had ever done—and if our story was indeed unique, the astronomy professor would give us a nickel.

When it was my turn, I said, "I washed and braided cow's tails at the county fair."

This was more or less true. My high school boyfriend was in Future Farmers of America and the previous summer, I'd hung around the show barns and helped out a bit with his sheep and his Jerseys.

My story was the show-stopper. I was henceforth considered a farm girl by a majority of students who had come from private high schools in Seattle and Portland.

("Private school" was the term used in the northwest for "college preparatory high school." Until I moved to New York in 1979, I only understood the word "prep" as slang for "prepare"—specifically, to prepare or be prepared for surgery, which I understood as a nurse shaving your pubic hair. Shortly after I settled in New York, I rode a Metro

North commuter train into Grand Central Station. What had been a pleasant discussion about the computer industry suddenly took a weird turn when the gentleman I had just met said, "Very interesting. Where did you prep?" I was nonplussed. He wanted to know my medical history? Four years earlier, I'd given birth to Max via a Caesarean section. "Cedars of Lebanon," I said awkwardly. He nodded and the conversation ended.)

By the time I'd worked for years in Manhattan, I'd edited the details of my rural past to such a fine point I'd convinced even myself that I was an expert on farm life. In conversations over *nouvelle cuisine* lunches, I tossed around arcane information, such as Guernseys are orange, Jerseys are brown. In New York City, this is a Nobel-Prize-winning ag background.

My agricultural personality props had to be swiftly discarded when I moved back to Ferndale in 1993. There is no one in the Eel River Valley who would support my farm girl persona.

Even my vocabulary had to be revised. George and Hazel referred to their acreage as "the ranch."

"I have inherited a ranch in California," I told people as I drove west across the continent, and they said, "How many acres?" When I said eighty, they threw me out in the snow to die.

"That's not a ranch! That's an apartment!"

Chastized, I reached the coast saying, "family farm."

"Dairy? Crops?"

Well, no. Paolo Gabrielli had built a dairy on the ranch. He had a barn, a corral, sheds, a chicken house with a below-ground still for *grappa*, and seven cows. On the hillside, he grew carrots for feed.

His barn and outbuildings are gone. George and Hazel and their friends tore them down and used the immortal redwood to build the new house.

I lived on a farm that was cow-free, until 1999, when I married John Lestina, a Czech—one-hundred-percent

Bohemian—from Minnesota. He'd been a computer systems analyst; in Ferndale, he became the manager of the Ferndale Cow Testing Association. John fixed meters that attached to the milking machines, shipped milk samples to the labs, and talked to experts from the Dairy Herd Improvement Association.

"Maybe we should have a few cows," he said. "Or at least one."

A cow. We had a house and a garden, and I have rosy cheeks.

The hitchhiker on the road to Guaymas had given Dan and me the key to happiness and I'd thrown it away.

Before I did, Dan and I returned to Los Angeles from Mexico. The sky was clear, the sun was bright, and the looters and SWAT teams were elsewhere.

Two letters awaited us.

One was from Bob Forest, the editor of *Datamation*, a computer trade magazine. His letter said to please call as soon as I returned from Mexico. Pending an interview, they were holding the Girl Friday job open for me.

The second letter was from Dan's father.

"Call collect as soon as you get in. We're so relieved you were able to leave during the riots."

Riots?

"I guess it was something unusual," I said.

Five years later, Dan and I were divorced, my name was on the *Datamation* masthead as an assistant editor, and I lived in Pasadena.

One Sunday, James, a man I was dating, invited me to his apartment to watch football. He owned an impressive 21-inch RCA color television.

"This must have cost you a fortune," I said.

"Not hardly," he said. "I carried it on my back out of a store on South Vermont during the riots."

WASHING CLOTHES

I didn't own a washing machine during the years I was married to Dan. I did laundry after work, after dinner, and after I did the dishes by myself while Dan watched television and lifted weights.

(To be fair, I didn't do the dishes every night. Sometimes I didn't even wash dishes every two nights. Or three. Dan was exasperated. I was exhausted.

One day outside an appliance store, I saw a portable dishwasher for $95.

"Let's get one!" I said to Dan, and Dan, never quick to voice an unpondered decision, finally said, "Tell you what. If you do the dishes right after dinner every night for a year, I'll buy you a portable dishwasher.")

The night laundromat was in the not-yet-fashionable Silver Lake region of Los Angeles and was populated with tired working women, often accompanied by small children in pajamas who would curl up near the warmth of a dryer and fall asleep.

The best nights were when two women came together, sisters-in-law I think they were. They were hilarious and loud. You can be loud in a laundromat and no one cares; the comforting sound of a mother's laughter rarely awakens a sleeping toddler.

Sometimes I complained to these women about my job, my husband, how tired I was. The women—they were old, probably close to 40—gave advice that has only increased in value.

I would recount an incident and Charlene would put her hands on her hips and say, "Honey, that ain't right. Listen to this, Elaine." I'd repeat the story and let the indignation conflagration begin. There is no better short-term therapy than trashing your current nemesis with strangers in a laundromat.

During that era, the Whitman alumni grapevine carried another laundromat story, this one about Gayle and Dave, two people from our college who had married in 1963 and moved to New Orleans where Dave was to attend medical school.

In NOLA, they lived in a typical poor-student neighborhood. Shortly after their arrival, Gayle took a week's load of dirty clothes to the nearby laundromat and was starting to load Dave's jeans when she saw the sign "Whites Only."

Gayle changed her laundry schedule and washed clothes only very late at night. She hovered over the washers as she put the clothes in, and hovered over as she removed them. She stood in front of the dryer without moving so no one could see the red and black and blue items flying past the foggy round window. She did this for nearly a year until the night she noticed a new sign had been posted near the original one. It said: "Maids in Uniform Excepted."

More recently, John and I were in the Turkish Republic of Northern Cyprus, a country the U.S. does not recognize, but the World Poker Tour does. John had won an online tournament, the prize for which was a trip to Cyprus, nine days at a five-star resort, and a place at the table of a WPT tournament.

We went to Cyprus ten days in advance of the tournament. I insisted that he not be jetlagged for the nine-hours-a-day of concentrated play. After a week or so, we moved to the resort where his win covered our lodging, but not our laundering—which, according to the price list, was spendy.

No problem, I said, I'll just go to a laundromat.

From 1878-1914 Cyprus was part of the British Empire, so even nearly a century later, Cypriots speak English.

"Where are you going?" the cab driver asked, and I explained I needed to wash dirty clothes. He stopped at a fluff-and-fold. I said, no, I didn't need to pay someone else to wash my clothes. See? I had my own soap.

A fifteen-minute-conversation ensued. I tried to describe what a laundromat was and the driver argued with me.

Finally, his bafflement turned to shocked disbelief.

"You are saying that in *America*"—the driver turned around and faced me fully, even though he had not stopped driving—"in *America* there are women who do not have washing machines inside their own houses?"

"Yes," I said. "That's not unusual. That's common."

A tiny segment of the tectonic plates of global idealism collided and shifted.

He said, "Here, in this country, every woman, *every woman,* has a washing machine in her house. We would never ask our wives and our mothers to do such a thing as you are doing."

As it should be. If the women ever got together late at night over a warm mess of unfolded clothes, for sure someone would have a story to tell and someone else would say, "Honey, that ain't right," and that would be the revolution from which there is no return.

UPROOTING

I wrote November 13 at the top of a page in my daybook and as I did, the bell-ringer in my brain raced to the tower. Today is a meaningful day…because? Is it the anniversary of my marriage to Clark, the father of my son?

That can't be right. Even in the '70s or, perhaps, especially in the '70s, I wouldn't have married someone on the thirteenth. I'd already laughed in the face of primitive superstition in 1964, when I'd married Dan on June 13.

Ah. November 13 is the day I *left* Dan.

Dan was, and probably still is—we haven't seen each other since December 1970, when a brief meeting was required to sign income-tax papers—a smart, funny man, kind, responsible and loyal. He was an engineer who wanted a pleasant wife, a couple of happy children, and an uneventful life not far from the mountains where we could ski, camp, and ride motorcycles.

A life as a wife and mother who took care of her family in a comfortable house in the suburbs, who wasn't required to have full-time employment, and who spent vacations wandering in the woods or sliding down snow-encrusted mountains was, to me, a literal nightmare.

A year or so before we separated, I began to have a recurrent dream in which Dan and I were sitting on a brown hillside. Below was a rushing river, and in the river were people riding on rafts and inner-tubes, splashing and laughing. They waved at us to join them. When I moved to do so, I discovered that I was a plant. My hands were gnarled and woody. I was rooted to the hot, dry ground. The only word I could hear was *withering*.

I could not settle down. "Settle down" was my mother's initial shot of discipline, a warning. I was talking too much, too loudly, laughing boisterously, expressing anger or frustration or excitement. *Settle down*, a crushing negative, the end of fun.

Simultaneously, paradoxically, the concept of settling down, getting married, having a family and keeping house (all after graduating from college and having a two-year "career") was presented as the ideal female objective. What could be more interesting than going from one house where my personality had to be straightened along with my teeth to another house in which I would spend a life secured with invisible braces to protect me from worst of all consequences, that of making a spectacle of myself?

And then there was Johnny. How could I tell Dan or anyone else that I was not only living my own life, I was also spiritually charged with living for my father? It wasn't a choice I had made in a child's moment of fantasy or with an adolescent's gothic romanticism. The command that I was not to "waste my life" was as clear to me as his request from the river bar.

My grandmother—so my mother and my aunt reported—believed simply and without embellishments in all things spiritual that would pass the Baptist test. This belief included communication with loved ones from the afterlife.

For three days when I was 16 months old, I uncharacteristically began crying and screaming. I refused to be left alone. At night, with the lights on, my mother and

Hazel took turns sitting by my crib. Dr. McKee made a house call to check on me. No fever, no signs of illness.

"She's teething," he said. "It will pass."

Ten days later, Mr. Kukuk, the manager of the telephone company, knocked on our door at supper time. My mother and Hazel were eating dinner. ("Creamed tuna on toast points," my mother says.) When my mother answered the door, Mr. Kukuk said, "Is your sister home?"

My mother returned to the kitchen and Hazel went to the front door. Mr. Kukuk was a neighbor, and, as Hazel was editing the *Enterprise* while George was in the Army, Mr. Kukuk could have been there on a town issue, something for the Chamber of Commerce.

She said, "Good evening," and Mr. Kukuk said, "I have a telegram."

She opened the door and motioned for him to come into the living room. He did, but he could no longer speak. He sat down and removed his hat. When he did, the gesture was the message.

"How bad is it?" Hazel whispered.

He shook his head, and once he starting shaking he couldn't stop. He handed her the yellow envelope and stood up. She showed him to the door and followed him out to the porch, watching as he walked down the street, his heavy shoulders slumped and his head still shaking.

Hazel returned to the kitchen and placed the telegram on the table. Neither woman spoke. A moment passed. Suddenly, they both ran upstairs. Hazel pulled me from the crib, and my mother held me as she walked back downstairs into the living room and sat in the rocking chair.

Hazel opened the telegram.

"He was killed on May twenty-fourth," she said. "When Wendy had that spell."

I say I've never seen my father, but my father has seen me. He saw me, and he used those three days to transmit his urgent message: *live a big life, as big as you can make it, big enough for both of us.*

33

In our final can-it-be-fixed? late-night talk, Dan promised me that if I stayed, I would never want for anything. At that point, his determination to save our marriage was based less on boundless love than on an unwillingness to carry the social scar of divorce.

I rejected his efforts, and cried, "I *want* to suffer!"

It was November 1969, and we had been married for five-and-a-half years. A month earlier I had begun a new job as the director of the Volunteer Bureau of Pasadena, a United Way agency housed in a green clapboard house sheltered by an oak grove. The Volunteer Bureau shared the house with the Foothill Planning Council and a community action program funded by the federal War on Poverty.

My job was to recruit and place volunteers for public and private nonprofit agencies in the San Gabriel Valley. I was new to social welfare. I'd left *Datamation* in a righteous fervor. Everyone I knew under 30 was doing something to save the world and I was writing about disk drives and random-access memory.

I was missing the revolution. While my colleagues protested the war in Vietnam, smoked marijuana, went to rock concerts, and slept with each other, I studied *Gourmet* magazine, read Julia Child and cooked. (I experimented so often that once after dinner I asked Dan, "Did you like it?" and he said "What difference does it make? We'll never have it again.")

In Pasadena, in the world of social welfare, I found my social niche. There, in that clapboard warren of offices, I was introduced to dedicated activists who not only shared my political values—they were fierce, passionate cooks.

One of my new friends was Ralph, an instructor of social work at USC. Although a few years older than I, Ralph was still safely under 30 and therefore could be trusted.

One day, we went to lunch. Ralph talked about his recent trip to South America and I said things weren't going too well in my marriage.

"Let me know if I can do anything to help," Ralph said, and quickly returned to the wonders of Chile.

Two days later, on the evening of November 13, I found Ralph's address in the phone book, walked up the stairs to the second floor of a pink stucco apartment building, and knocked on the door. I was carrying a white Samsonite suitcase, a high school graduation gift from my mother and Doc. Inside the suitcase were four changes of clothes, a Scrabble board, and a Bible.

Ralph answered the door in a bathrobe.

"Hi," I said. "I've left Dan. Can I sleep on your couch?"

I stayed a month. Most evenings we cooked spaghetti *carbonara* and drank Almaden Mountain Rhine, after which I would pull out the sofa-bed and drift off in a giddiness of independence.

Discretion not being the better part of valor or of any other part of my life at the time, the Volunteer Bureau's board of directors, all of whom were members of the Junior League, soon learned that there had been an abrupt change in my marital status.

Two women were assigned to confront me. They entered my office, shut the door, and looked around to make themselves comfortable. The office held two chairs, and I was sitting in one of them.

The elder of the two—because of Junior League bylaws neither could have been over 40; to me, they were faded flowers—sat down opposite me.

"We are concerned," she said, "that you are living with Ralph."

"Yes," I said. "Well, not 'with' really, more like 'at.'"

"Your behavior does not reflect appropriately on the Volunteer Bureau," the standing member said, carefully, in a cadence that revealed memorization.

"I had a sort of emergency," I said. "Ralph has been kind enough to let me sleep on his couch until I can find my own place. I haven't been able to find one I can afford, so it is taking more time than I expected."

"We can fix that," said the stander.

The next day, with the help of their help, I moved into a mother-in-law house behind an elegant craftsman bungalow five blocks from my job.

There I began my chosen path of suffering.

Turns out, I wasn't very good at it. A historical view of human existence would grant me, at best, a 1.5 on a 10-point scale of suffering, and even that rating declines as age delivers humility.

Ralph never married. He worked in city planning and community development, he wrote grants for innovative social programs and when the money came, he implemented the programs. He created leaders beneath him, he shared the power, he sidestepped the limelight. When he retired, speeches attesting to his accomplishments, his creativity and his generosity were given by former gang members and Hispanic mothers, by mayors and corporate executives, by Episcopal priests and artists and philanthropists—all people Ralph had inspired to risk their resources and their lives to make the world a better place for their children.

When Ralph wasn't working, he was traveling, taking long trips to frequently dangerous places. Sometimes, places got dangerous after he got there, like the time he was with a tour guide in Israel on a hill overlooking a desert.

"Who are all those people?" Ralph asked, pointing to a long line on the horizon. "What is this, rush hour?"

The guide grabbed the binoculars, uttered something primal, and turned around.

"We have to leave. Now. That's the army. They're invading Lebanon."

The first Christmas I was separated from Dan, Ralph, who had a month's holiday, went to Russia. I went to Ferndale to be the matron of honor in the wedding of Janet Crane. My responsibilities were to be pretty, smile, and read aloud the 13th Chapter of 1st Corinthians.

"If I speak in the tongues of men or of angels, but do not have love, I am only a resounding gong or a clanging cymbal," I read.

Janet was married in front of the massive river-rock fireplace in her parents' living room. It was a small wedding and from my position at the front, I could see every face in the room.

"...if I have a faith that can move mountains, but do not have love, I am nothing," I continued. Hazel was shaking her head and biting her lip. My face began to ache.

"Love is patient, love is kind...it does not dishonor others, it is not self-seeking, it is not easily angered, it keeps no record of wrongs."

My mother was standing in the back, in a darkened corner between two perpendicular pianos. Her mouth formed a single hard line that seemed to run mandible to mandible. Janet, who had been my friend since we were both three, was the daughter of the doctor who had employed my mother after she was widowed. The doctor's daughter was getting married and her daughter was getting a divorce. She wasn't shamed. She was mainlining the sorrow I was pouring into the room.

"Love never fails..." The thumping lump in my chest moved into my throat. "Where there are prophecies, they will cease..." I was losing control over my voice.

"Love always protects, always trusts, always hopes, always perseveres..." Tears were coming and this was an unfamiliar translation of the scripture. I said "preserves."

I brushed my right hand over my eyes to keep the tears out so I could continue reading. My hand turned black from dissolving mascara.

"When I was a child, I talked like a child, I thought like a child, I reasoned like a child..." My voice collapsed. I was not suppressing tears, I was suppressing sobs, the big kind, the kind that make your nose run. Globs of moisture dropped on my green taffeta bridesmaid dress.

"...and the greatest of these is love."

Janet glared at me.

A year later, Ralph said, "What are your plans for Christmas? Going to Ferndale?" I said no, spending two weeks surrounded by disappointed faces was not my first choice. Ralph said he was flying to Libya to visit a friend who was a diplomat.

I went home and opened the new issue of *Sunset* magazine. A full-page ad with a photograph of a green mountain rising from white sand said, "Come to Peru."

The next day, I walked into a bank and was given a loan for $500.

"I'm going to Peru for Christmas," I told Ralph, and he said, "Great! I've never been there."

He left a week before I did. When I arrived at the Lima airport, he met me wearing the loose pants of the Quechuans and an immense, woven poncho.

"How do you like my clothes?" he yelled. "I sold my stuff on the black market!"

In the last few days of my two weeks in Peru, we traveled into the Andes to see the Inca ruins at Machu Picchu. We stayed in the village of Cuzco.

One very cold and very dark night—there's no ambient light at 11,000 feet—in a drenching downpour, we chose to eat dinner at the Arizona Café, a tiny restaurant across a cobbled street from the bus station. The décor was a moldy mix of black and white animal hides nailed to the walls. The only other customers were five or six Quechan men who were leaning on a bar, talking and drinking.

The menu was a mix of local food and "Italian." In a complete leave of travel commonsense, I ordered spaghetti and was served a platter of noodles covered with catsup.

Ralph the wise selected the local *criollo* with chicken and cilantro and lots of garlic, a fragrant, steaming soup that he did not share.

Our table was in the center of the room. Ralph sat facing me, his back to the door. He did not see the bus pull into the station or, shortly thereafter, the screen door of the Arizona swing open to admit a tall blonde woman in a Bavarian peasant dress, holding the hand of a black toddler.

"Hey," I said to Ralph, "another American just came in."

He turned around, snapped his head back and hissed at me. "I know that girl. I went to high school with her. I can't stand her. Pretend you don't see her."

"Ralph!" the woman screamed.

I went back to Pasadena and Ralph stayed in Peru with his new best friend and her little boy. When we last told and retold the old stories, Ralph said the woman reappeared in his life several more times over the years, and that he now found her "pleasant."

If we live long enough, we can overcome even high school.

FAMILY LOAN

Ralph was not the only friend I made during the four years I worked in the clapboard house of community organizers. Ralph's student, Sara, a citizen of Scotland who was getting her master's degree in Social Work from USC, was one, and so was Mattie, the secretary to the boss of the planning agency.

And then there was Giuliana.

A month older than I, Giuliana was born in the mountains of Abruzzi, to which her Roman mother and sister had fled when her father deemed them in danger from both sides of the war. Giuli, according to her sister Paola— who has yet to find sustainable peace on this issue— refused to feed herself, and was, Paola insists, hand-fed by their mother "with silver spoons" until she was nine.

However she received nourishment, Giuli was, by the age of nine, a resident of Venezuela. Her father moved the family to South America after the war, and there her mother ran the cafeteria in the American compound of Standard Oil. Eventually, her parents moved to San Francisco, and after college in Venezuela, Giuli came to America to get a master's degree in social work from San Diego State. That task accomplished, she found a job at the Foothill Planning Council in the green clapboard house, thanks to the networking of her mother, who met Ralph's mother in a doctor's office in San Francisco.

In the fall of 1970, on the first day of her first professional job, Giuliana drove into the parking lot and crashed her Toyota Corona Mark II into the wooden back stairs of the green clapboard building.

We were friends before lunch.

Giuli told me she'd rented a cottage and she didn't have any furniture. I said I had too much furniture and that she was welcome to anything she needed, on family loan. Family loan means, this is yours forever until, or if, I want it back.

She chose my set of wicker sofa and chairs from the Ferndale Village Club, a red Oriental rug that was a hand-me-down from Dan's sister, and a black American primitive armoire and a 1922 Spartan console radio, both of which I'd purchased for $10 each from a couple who were divesting themselves of tangibles to seek a higher plane of sensual awareness. The radio didn't work but that wasn't the point: it was a beauty, standing tall, its rounded corners finished in a wavy grained Art Deco veneer.

Giuliana filled her half of a duplex with the family loan and went to the Handlebars Saloon for a beer with a visiting cousin. In the crowd at the tavern were two Hungarians, Sandor and his friend, Hugo.

"There's a couple of cute ones," Hugo said. "Listen to them talk! Do you speak Spanish?"

Sandor tuned in. "That's not Spanish!" he said. "That's Italian!"

Sandor—Sandy—had lived in Italy for a few years after he had been forced to leave Hungary in a hurry during the revolution of October, 1956, when he was 16 and had been photographed by the Russians throwing rocks at their soldiers.

"We were trying to break into the jails, to free political prisoners," he told us. "We were so stupid we didn't know they had cameras. We knew they had guns. A friend and I were throwing rocks, and I hear this sound next to me, like a

Pop! Pop! I turn around, my friend's head is on the ground. They blew his head off. I ran like hell. Took a bit of shrapnel in my foot, not a big deal. Next night, a man who had been a friend of my father's"—his father had been forced into the German army, sent to the Russian front and was never again heard from—"this man came to the house, and he said to my mother that I had to leave that night, that my name was on a list and I would be arrested in the morning."

After dark, Sandy, with a small bag of possessions, walked across a snowy field and into some woods where a large group of refugees, mostly men, had gathered to head *en masse* to the Austrian border a few miles distant on the other side of the Einser Canal. Crossing the canal next to the village of Andau was a narrow wooden bridge, the only place of passage. Russian patrols and their proxy Hungarian troops guarded the bridge.

"We appeared at the bridge," Sandy said, "and there were two Russian soldiers there. Two guys with guns. There were eighty of us, some were veterans of the war, some had guns, too, I think. They were desperate. Those two guys looked at us, then they just walked back into the guard house and let us pass. I guess they figured they didn't have a chance, and they didn't have the fight in them, you know, they were just doing a job."

In Austria, Sandy was offered a relocation to Italy.

"That was easy. I'd seen the postcards, blue skies, the Mediterranean, Gina Lollobrigida. I went to Italy, you bet."

He was in Italy for five years and had applied for visas to the United States and Australia. The American visa, offering permanent political asylum, arrived first.

Sandy moved to New York and married a nurse. They had four children before she was diagnosed with a severe mental illness. To aid the family in settling in an environment less stressful than New York, Catholic Charities moved the family to California, but his wife did not recover. She was admitted to a state hospital and the marriage was dissolved.

By the winter of 1972, the chance to speak Italian to a beautiful woman at the Handlebars Saloon was a welcome development.

Giuli invited Sandy to her duplex. He looked around and said, "Why do you have a radio that doesn't work? That makes no sense to me." He fixed it.

A month later they were engaged.

"I am wondering what to get them for a wedding present," I said to Sara.

Sara, characteristically, was careful in her response. "I'm supposed to tell you that all they want is the radio."

Sandy and Giuli are still married—an anomaly among my friends—and the family loan radio stands proudly in their entry hall. It's the first thing I see when I walk into their house.

In my closet is a rust-colored shawl that belongs to Sara. I borrowed it to stay warm at Sandy and Giuli's outdoor wedding reception.

I have no intention of returning it.

FULL CIRCLE TABLE

I bought a house in October 1970, when I was 26.

After Dan and I agreed to end our marriage, I rented a two-bedroom cottage built in 1925 on Penn Street in Pasadena.

Penn Street is north of Washington and west of Los Robles. The coordinates refer to a neighborhood where the pavement buckles from bulging roots of old walnut trees that embrace each other like weary women over the narrow streets.

The coordinates are code for the demographics, a map for redlining, which is a term I learned when I received a telephone installation bill for $300.

Pacific Telephone's offices were in downtown Pasadena. On a lunch break from the Volunteer Bureau, I walked in with my bill. I'd had a telephone in my name in southern California in four different residences in five years and installation had never cost more than about $30.

A clerk smiled at me, looked up my records as a Pacific Telephone customer, and said, "Yes, there's been a mistake." The bill was corrected to an amount in the thirty-dollar range. I bought a ham sandwich at Stottlemeyer's and went back to work.

"Did you get your telephone bill settled?" Ralph asked. I said, "Yes. They must have confused me with someone else."

"Don't kid yourself," he said. "You wouldn't have gotten the reduction if you hadn't gone in person. How long did it take them to find your records?"

I tried to recreate the scene. I'd been chatting, telling the Pacific Bell clerk about my marriage breaking up, the usual topic women share in chance encounters with strangers.

"There's a different price structure for blacks!" Ralph was shouting to shatter what he regarded as intolerable naiveté. "Your address is red-lined! Everything costs more when you're poor and you're black!"

Much of the housing in the northwest section of Pasadena had been constructed with money from the coffers of post-World War I industrialists from Cleveland and Detroit, Chicago and Pittsburgh, wealthy individuals who wintered among the orange groves nestled against the San Gabriel Mountains. The cottages on Penn Street and the surrounding neighborhoods were modest houses built for the help, servants who worked for the snowbirds when they were in town.

Low-income housing was gracious in those days. The house I rented was well-built and set back from the street behind a tidy lawn on a generous lot. The back yard was shaded by a mature avocado tree.

On my block there were sixteen houses. A Mexican woman with three children lived on one corner. A Japanese family with five children lived across the street. When I moved to Penn Street, a young white man lived down the block. He had moved there to establish residency in order to run for Congress.

Everyone else was black.

That fact was not incidental in my decision to rent on Penn Street. Ralph was friends with the would-be Congressman and one day when my friends and I had gathered to develop new tactics in the social revolution we were sure was changing the world soon and forever, Ralph, referring to the campaigning candidate, said, "He's a blockbuster! We should all do that! We should all buy houses in Northwest Pasadena and integrate the neighborhoods!"

It was a stirring proposal, and it coincided with my need to find a place to live. I drove north of Washington and west of Los Robles and spotted the "For Rent" on Penn Street.

I moved there within a week.

Shortly thereafter, Ralph changed tactics, and rented instead an architecturally significant house-behind-a-house on South Orange Grove Avenue, not far from the Rose Parade's headquarters in the Wrigley mansion—not at all Northwest Pasadena. Everyone else made similar choices. The blockbusting candidate lost the election and moved, leaving me, as far as I was ever able to determine, the only person of Anglo-Saxon ethnicity in my census tract.

Before we separated, Dan had inherited enough furniture from his grandmother to fill a much larger apartment, and he was eager to dispose of the random pieces we had acquired—an algae-green sofa, a hutch Hazel no longer wanted, and a chest of drawers my aunt Jeanne said was ugly.

The interior of the Penn Street house had been freshly painted beige and a new gold shag carpet had been installed throughout its 1,100 square feet. Two gardeners who were retained by the owner came by and mowed the lawn. Sometimes I watched them from the comfort of a plastic chair on the shaded front porch. Two other renters lived in the backyard. A single man who worked for the Los Angeles Public Schools lived in the one-bedroom apartment that extended over the double garage; a single woman who ran the Outward Bound program for the Pasadena City Schools lived in a studio alongside the garage.

"They've lived here a long time," the landlord said. "Please respect them."

I wasn't insulted. I knew exactly the pandemonium I could, with little effort, attract and unleash.

Two months after I moved in, I came home from work, parked my car in front of the house, and my heart fell.

On the lawn was a red *For Sale* sign. In big black letters was a scrawled telephone number.

It felt like an eviction notice, a message to the rest of the folks on the street: "Temporary housing of transient chick. Real people to come."

I went inside (through an unlocked door; in the six years I was to live there, I never used the house key), and dialed the number that was on the sign.

"How much does it cost?" I asked. The owner, who was also my landlord and the real estate agent, said, "Twenty-four thousand dollars."

"Okay," I said.

I did call Ferndale and asked Doc's opinion. It was the last time I ever accessed that resource.

He said, "I wouldn't do it, Wendy. Some day you may marry again and the man you may meet and may marry may not want to live there."

What he should have said was, "That's the asking price. Offer them $15,000 and see what happens." (Several years later, the tenant in the one-bedroom told me the owner had offered him the property for $17,000.)

The seller was skeptical that a young woman could afford to buy a house.

"What is your income?" he asked.

I worked two jobs. During the day, I was the director of the Volunteer Bureau; in the evening, I researched and wrote an investment newsletter for *Datamation*'s high-end readers.

(When I told the editor-in-chief, Bob Forest, that I was quitting my job, leaving *Datamation* to "do something I believe in," he said that my plan was noble, although sometimes, "things you believe in don't often pay the bills." He suggested that I take over the newsletter, a promotional tool of the sales department filled with thinly disguised investment advice. From me, the expert. The entirety of my investment experience was buying six shares of Ross Perot's Electronic Data Systems at its initial offering price and selling it a year later when it had increased several hundred percent. I used the profits to buy Dan and me matching motorcycles.)

Datamation paid me $400 a month, and the Volunteer Bureau, $500.

"I make $900 a month," I said, and the real estate agent said, "Terrific! You'll have no problem getting a mortgage."

After a down payment of $4,000 (from the $10,000 I'd been given when I turned 21 and was eligible to receive Johnny's World War II death benefit), my mortgage payment was $130. The two rental units brought in $210 a month.

I had positive cash flow. What I didn't have was a dining room table.

Downtown Pasadena, not the hip Old Town it is today, was home to seedy bars, grimy barber shops, and antique stores where "consignment" meant "pawn."

My favorite pawn shop was Arnie's. He had cool stuff like anti-daylight savings campaign buttons.

I told Arnie I needed a dining room table.

He had just the ticket, a round table, five-and-a half feet in diameter, with an ornately carved base.

"Check this out," he said, and he reached under the table, tugged on two wooden slats, and shoved the top. It tilted, creating a huge circular target with carved feet.

"How come the wood is two colors?" I asked, and he said, "The top is teak. The base is rosewood. I don't know how old it is, but look, it's all handmade, and these kinds of screws, they're not foundry made. This kind of work, it's not from this century."

I couldn't pay the $300 asking price in one shot. I made a down payment and after four installments it was mine.

The thing about the tilt-top table is that in the 44 years since I purchased it, I've only lived in one house, briefly, where it fit. It's not only immense in diameter, it is too high. Sitting in an ordinary kitchen chair, even an adult is hit in the sternum.

In 1997, I had the table top refinished. When the refinisher picked it up, he asked how I wanted it to look. I said please keep it as it is, a teak top and a rosewood base.

He returned it a rich dark red overall, the color of the base.

"I don't know who told you it was a teak top," he said. "It's all rosewood."

In 2007, I rented an office in Ferndale's renovated creamery building, where the tilt-top table created an instant conference room. The office was spacious enough for its grandeur. As the job matured, however, I was able to avoid more and more meetings. John good-naturedly hauled it home and stored it in the laundry room, where it served as a clothes-folding table.

It was a dining table that seated eight people. Who has that much washing? Certainly not the two of us. It's only a thing, I reminded myself. And we need the money. Do I want to keep the table or the ranch?

I called the auction yard in Eureka and Don Johnson, the owner, drove down in a truck to pick it up. He was skeptical about his worth. He appreciated the provenance, he said, but he wasn't confident about selling it at a decent price.

"Young people, and that's who our furniture buyers are—senior citizens aren't buying furniture, like you, they're getting rid of stuff—young people aren't looking for pieces like this," he said. "It's too big, too dark, too heavy. They want mid-century. *Twentieth* century. Our hot items lately were a gold velvet sectional and some lava lamps."

"I can't believe you're selling it," John had said. "Isn't it the first piece of furniture you ever bought?"

I had said all the right things: about downsizing, being realistic, finding a new home where it will be more comfortable, learning to let go, some people lose everything in fires and floods.

Yet, in the morning, before Don Johnson arrived, I'd crept into the laundry room, placed my hand on the solid teak-or-maybe-rosewood top and let the soundtrack of four decades of an often complicated domestic life stream through my soul until my throat ached.

Five children had eaten and played games and studied at that table. Five children had made valentines with Crazy Glue that dripped and cut steak with knives that slipped; they'd been bored or angry or hurt and had carved chinks in the sides. My son Max had lorded over the table with the advantage of a high chair; Solange and Zoe, sisters who were foster placements from Los Angeles County, learned to set a beautiful table—and used the height advantage to surreptitiously drop unfamiliar food into their laps. And that table was the family center of my life with Kevin and Anita.

I met Anita and her older brother, Kevin, when I was married to Dan. At the urging of my boss, Bob Forest, I was acting with a theater group in Sierra Madre, a small town adjacent to Pasadena. There, I took acting lessons taught by Florence MacMichael, an actress who was reaping residuals she'd earned playing Wilbur Post's neighbor in the talking-horse sitcom "Mr. Ed."

At one rehearsal, another actor who owned an increasing number of low-income rentals, remarked that one of his tenants was delinquent with the rent. The landlord was nervous about making a personal call to collect.

I was scornful. "You're afraid of black people?!"

"I am when they're bigger than I am," he said.

I said, "Give me the address."

I drove slowly down Mountain Avenue in Duarte, east of Pasadena, reading the numbers on the houses. As I reached the address, I came upon two partially clad preschool children playing in the middle of the street.

I pulled over to the side of the road and called to them.

"Where's your mother?" I asked. The boy said she didn't live there anymore and that his father was at work. A babysitter, he said, was inside the house.

The babysitter was watching television. She was 12.

"If you want something, call their grandma," she said, and handed me a Pasadena number.

I found a grocery bag, filled it with a few items of clothing, settled Kevin and Anita in my car and drove back to Los Angeles, to a bemused Dan. I called the children's grandmother.

"My name is Wendy," I said. "I found Kevin and Anita playing half-dressed in the middle of Mountain Avenue, no grown-up in charge. I brought them home with me."

"That's a good thing," Grandma said—I was never to call her by any other name—"I'll tell James where they at."

James was six months older than I, a man of medium height and muscular build. He *was* bigger than his landlord. He had more than one personality and the ability to call to the fore whichever one was most effective for the moment. When we met, he was the apologetic, concerned, and wronged father.

"Cheri, their mother, is in prison for parole violations. She can't take care of the kids. She has a drug problem. Heroin. When she gets out this time, she has to find another place to live. I guess I'm going to have to find another babysitter."

Until that day I had had no interest in children, except perhaps as employees. My two younger sisters and their friends cleaned my bedroom on Saturdays in exchange for penny candy and plastic miniature animals. Children were little kids and I was a big kid and that was a universal caste system I favored.

Now I made an abrupt change. I became, if not the babysitter, the person responsible for a babysitter. Every day for a year Kevin and Anita were with me for some period of time. Predictably, my life diverged dramatically from Dan's life, which was focused on completing his engineering degree at USC.

When Cheri was released from prison, James went to jail. While she'd been incarcerated, he'd been visited by the police for some outstanding traffic warrants, and while they were hanging around his garage, they noticed some stolen car parts.

That story is not only distorted by 47 years of incoming data. That story *began* distorted. I have no clue where to begin to unravel to the truth, so I will only report what I do know.

James went to jail, to Biscailuz Center on top of a hill in East Los Angeles. It was his first offense, and he had a family to support, so his six-month sentence was modified to allow for work furlough. He could continue to work at a plastics extrusion factory in El Monte on graveyard shift, if he could find someone to drive him back and forth.

I was that someone. An exciting new grocery store had just opened in Pasadena near the *Datamation* offices. It was a wine and food importer called Trader Joe's. The store included a deli that made custom sandwiches. Five nights a week, I went to Trader Joe's at 8:00 p.m., bought sandwiches, fruit, and sodas, and made up James's lunch. At 11:00 p.m., I drove my Camaro up the hill and checked in with the guards. I had special privileges, granted by them to me because I brought them recent copies of *Hot Rod* and *Motor Trend*.

The guards paged James, he was escorted to the front, and we left for El Monte. Eight hours after I left him at the plastics factory, I picked him up, with breakfast food, and drove him back to Biscailuz Center.

During this time, I left Dan.

A year later, after Cheri moved in with her pimp and she and James were divorced, James, Kevin and Anita moved into the house on Penn Street.

I remember, not necessarily in this order, coming into the house and finding Kevin and Anita sitting in front of the refrigerator on the little chairs that had once belonged to a fancy set of children's furniture that a would-be suitor had given my widowed mother. The refrigerator door was open. They were staring at the contents as if it were a television program.

"What are you guys doing?" I asked, and Anita said, "We like to look at food."

I recall taking a bath, grabbing a moment when the house was quiet. The children were outside playing with the neighborhood kids. I ran more hot water, lay my head back and put a washcloth over my eyes.

Suddenly, there was conversation and activity. I moved the washcloth to more sensitive areas and opened my eyes. Four small faces were staring at me. The washcloth didn't cover much, but that didn't matter because no one was interested in my body.

"Wendy," Anita said. "Can we make Jell-O?"

Until a few months after they moved in, Kevin and Anita didn't let me take naps. I would lie on the sofa and drift away, and they would poke me, shout at me to wake up, and push up my eyelids.

"Tell them to let me doze off, please," I said to James, and he said, "They don't understand normal naps. They only know nodding, from heroin. It scares them."

The baggage of Cheri. She was tall, an inch or so taller than James, with dead white skin and a towering blonde hairpiece sprayed into a permanent beehive. Cheri was gaunt from heroin addiction. Her front teeth had been knocked out when she was 14 while in a California Youth Authority prison. I'd fixate on that cheap, unmatched bridge when she was threatening and ranting. Not that we saw her often. She didn't visit unless she had exhausted all other possibilities for cash.

Of course, she promised to visit often. She'd tell the children, as she folded a $20 bill into a swinging handbag, that'd she'd be back "Wednesday" to take them to Disneyland.

"Wednesday" never came.

"Is Wednesday tomorrow?" Kevin would ask. He would sit by the front door and wait. One night, I heard a noise in the living room and I got up to check. Kevin had stirred in his sleep—by the front door. I carried him back to his bed, but not before he asked me if he'd been asleep when Cheri had come.

Another time, when it was no longer "Wednesday," she banged on the door at 3:00 a.m. James opened it, and she stood outside, in the damp and cold, dressed in a silver miniskirt and a halter top. She was high, and she demanded to see the children.

Before James could get control of the situation, they were awake. Kevin, a first-grader, scrambled out of his bunk, ran into the living room, and grabbed Cheri around the ankles.

"Don't go, Mommy, don't go," he screamed. "We forgive you."

In the box of memorabilia from those years is a Mother's Day story, written at school by Kevin when he was seven. It says, "I have a real mother and a fake mother. I like my fake mother because she lets us make Jell-O."

I was their fake mother until a year or two after James and I were no longer a couple, and James's new girlfriend gave an ultimatum: I'm out of the picture or she is.

"Grace got mad at us," Anita told me, "because when we went to the food store, she bought junk and we said, 'Wendy says that's not real food.' So we can't be with you anymore."

On several instances after the children were forbidden to see me, I parked across the street from their school to catch a glimpse of them. When they saw me, they'd wave excitedly and then, furtively.

The depth of my grief was unexpected. No one had warned me how subtly children seize your soul.

I hadn't seen either child for several years by the time Kevin was 15 and had left James's house in Pasadena to move to South Central Los Angeles and become a Crip. Shortly after, Anita, 13, followed, looking for Cheri. She found her, and within weeks, Anita was addicted to drugs. She supported her habit by streetwalking.

Among my papers I have a file from the Pasadena Christian School that contains Anita's report cards. At six, she had mostly A's. Her teacher wrote that she was "happy, cheerful, eager to learn, the center of many friends, and a joy in the classroom."

Anita's mother has been dead for 30 years. I was living in New York when James called.

"Cheri passed," he said. "An intentional overdose. She was murdered."

Maybe, maybe not.

James died in 2012. Kevin robbed banks, sold drugs, and committed felonies while in federal prison, where he is now, where he has spent most of his adult life, and where he will stay until his parole in 2025, when he is 60.

Anita has survived. In the online guest book that was included in the newspaper obituary for James, Anita wrote, "I have had a ruff life & thank you daddy for never turning your back on me…"

I did turn my back. I did not contact either Kevin or Anita when I knew where they were. I did not loan them money the few times they asked.

I saw Anita only once after she was nine. She was 27 and had just been released from the county jail. She had stopped to see Grandma at the very moment when I was in Los Angeles on business and had decided, with no advance notice, to visit Grandma.

Anita and I sat outside on the red concrete steps under the clothesline.

"Why didn't you come for me?" she asked, "Why didn't you let me know where you were?"

I said, "I love you, but drugs have no place in my life. You have to make that choice."

It was a cheap line from self-help literature on tough love. What I couldn't, or didn't, say was: *I am living without a safety net. I am responsible for Max's and my survival. There is not enough of me to take risks, to be vulnerable to potential danger. I lock my doors.*

Don Johnson's skepticism was justified. Six months after I signed the tilt-top table over to the auction yard, he wheeled it back into my office. No one had wanted it, he said, not even for the $200 I had finally been willing to accept.

He helped me lower the top and adjust the wooden slats.

"I'm sorry," he said. "It really is a beautiful piece."

After he left, I stood by the stolid hunk of rosewood-whatever and smiled.

"So," I said. "It's not over."

.

ROAD TRIP

In the summer of 1973, Bob Forest dispatched me on a national three-city trip to survey the opinions of data-processing managers.

The first stop was Dallas. I arrived in the afternoon, checked into the Sheraton, and settled in my room to hand-write an article for another publication that was due in a few days. I would order dinner from room service, lay out my clothes for the following morning's interview and go to bed early.

I looked in the mirror. The woman who looked back at me, the one who doesn't like me as much as I like myself, screamed "What?! You're 29 years old, you're single, there are no men, no loves in your life, no one knows where you are or what you are doing. Lighten up! Go down to the bar and pick up some cowboy. No one gives a damn, believe me."

I'd rarely been in bars. I'd never gone into a bar alone and I'd never emerged from one with a man I'd just met.

I put on a pair of pink bell-bottomed pants and a pink-and-green top, packed a purse with an emergency novel, and walked into the Sheraton's bar. It was 4:30 p.m. The bar was empty. I sat down at a table for six and the barmaid took my order for a beer. I opened the novel.

Shortly before 5 p.m. a dozen suited men ambled in and seated themselves along the bar. They were middle-aged and well-fed, and they all sported a fluffy white flower in their lapels.

The barmaid reappeared.

"The gentleman at the end of the bar would like to buy you a drink," she said.

"What's that thing on their jackets?" I whispered.

"Cotton!" she said. "We've got a convention of cotton farmers here this week."

"Tell him thank you, but no," I said.

A long while passed, hours or maybe ten minutes, and another group of men poured in, these in golf shirts and khakis, younger and leaner. The room vibrated with their energy; none glanced in my direction.

"And who is this?" I asked the barmaid, when she brought me a second bowl of Chex mix.

"High school basketball coaches," she said. "From all over the southwest. We have another high school convention here, too. Home ec teachers. It's a busy week."

Not for the would-be pick-up artist. ("You're good-looking enough," a *Datamation* co-worker explained years later, "but a guy'd have to be totally tanked not to notice you eat glass.")

A third influx arrived with a third beer.

"Black morticians," the barmaid said. Off-limits, I knew. Texas is not Los Angeles.

Soon all the tables were filled except mine. I sat alone in an overcrowded saloon, conspicuous and embarrassed. As I reached for my purse to settle up, I was jostled by two guys who'd just walked in.

"Too bad if you're saving this for someone," one said, grabbing a chair and sitting on it backwards. "We're here now."

A second young man with a wry smile seated himself opposite me. I found him very funny and very cute. His name was Clark.

The next day, after the *Datamation* interview, I cancelled my flights to Oklahoma City and Denver, and Clark and I—and Teddy, his German shepherd—drove to the rest of my appointments in his rickety Mustang. To Oklahoma, to Colorado, and on to Las Vegas.

At one point Clark said, "I'm not sure the car will make it all the way to Pasadena," and I said, "Sure, it will. And if it doesn't, so what?"

The head gasket blew ten miles west of Vegas. The two of us and Teddy the dog stood on the side of the road with paws out. Before long, a married couple sharing driving shifts in a long-haul, eighteen-wheeler oil truck pulled over, packed us in the back behind the cab, and carried us to Long Beach.

It was 2 a.m. when they let us off near a refinery. I found a pay phone and called Sue Laris, my childhood friend from Ferndale who now lived in Southern California. Sue would, I assured Clark, be happy to drive her Volkswagen from Altadena to Long Beach in the middle of the night.

Sue showed up as quickly as could be expected.

"Mind if I smoke?" Clark asked.

"Yes," Sue said. "I do mind." She didn't say another word the rest of the way.

Sue recovered sufficiently to stand up for me at our wedding in Las Vegas three months later. The best man was the driver of the eighteen-wheeler.

Six months later, Clark and I decided another road trip was in order. We had no money; we'd quit our jobs shortly after we returned from Las Vegas.

Sue, who remembers these sorts of things, says that when she asked me why we quit our jobs, I said, "If we're working we're not together, and we got married to be together."

I had turned 30, and, suddenly, urgently, I wanted to have a baby. Sue and her husband Jim had a five-year-old son, Michael.

"I have an idea," I said to Sue after the wedding. "Let's both get pregnant and have children who can grow up together and be best friends."

Sue said okay, went home and got pregnant.

I didn't. It seemed I couldn't. So now it was August, her baby was due in two weeks, and I was leaving town in a dramatic exhibition of acute envy.

To raise money for the trip, I wrote letters to public relations people in the software development divisions of NCR and Xerox and hustled some on-the-road corporate newsletter writing jobs. The writing assignments would eventually net us $250: enough, we figured—accurately, as it turned out—to cover the gas on the Shell credit card.

To pay for lodging and food, we had two plans. One was to stay with as many relatives and friends as we could find, and the other was to drive from Pasadena to Ferndale, rent a U-Haul, clear out the attics and garages of my mother and Hazel, and return to Pasadena to hold a yard sale. Both plans worked splendidly. I promoted the yard sale with a classified ad in the Pasadena *Star-News*: "Heirs liquidating Northern California estate."

Arnie and several other antique dealers showed up at Penn Street before dawn. We sold everything, including my wedding dress and we grossed more than $500.

It was August 8, 1974. We cleaned up the yard and cheered with excitement as Richard Nixon appeared on our tiny black-and-white portable television to resign the presidency. The next morning, in a 1967 blue Chevelle loaded with camping gear and Teddy the dog, we left for America.

We stopped in Las Vegas. Our limit for the casinos was 15 cents. We each had three nickels for the slot machines and when that was gone—about an hour later—we left. We camped in Arizona, Utah, Colorado; then, we drove like hell to Tulsa, where Clark's brother Bob, an Amway distributor, lived in an immense new house.

Inviting ourselves—and Teddy—into Bob's home was not the most thoughtful plan. Unsurprisingly, he tired of us quickly, although it may not have been entirely because of Teddy. I was obsessed with the national news. While we were in Tulsa—Bob had a color television set—there was a story, later proved untrue, that the Pentagon had been anticipating a military coup by Nixon before he resigned.

I called Sue. The year before, she had watched the Senate Watergate hearings during the day and would call me at *Datamation* with regular updates ("There are tapes! They taped everything!")

Jim answered the phone. "The Pentagon thought Nixon was staging a coup!" I said, and Jim said, "We have a new baby boy. His name is Casey."

Clark and I drove on, camping in Hannibal, Missouri, along the Mississippi, and fishing for our dinner as a tribute to Mark Twain. Up to Chicago for a job. Over to Dayton, Ohio, for another job. Down to Economy, Indiana, to see the town where Clark was born, and over to Richmond, to stay with Kate, Clark's quarter-Blackfoot-Indian grandmother.

Clark hadn't seen Kate for years. She had been mean to them as kids, he said. She had a switch and she'd use it. He was afraid of her. And, he said, she didn't talk much.

"What did she say when you told her we were coming?" I asked, as we parked in front of her house.

"I didn't call ahead," Clark said.

Kate's house was a droopy, two-story wood frame structure that might have once been painted a light blue. Potted succulents filled the small porch, lined the railings, and grew in the worn seats of overstuffed chairs.

Clark knocked and the door opened immediately. She had been watching us.

"Grandma!" Clark said. "Do you know who I am?"

"Why wouldn't I?" she said. "You was always trouble, Clarky."

She invited us to come in.

"Put the dog in the back," she said. "Behind the fence."

Her house was clean, tidy, modest. There were a few decorative plates and some photographs. Everything seemed curated, as if only the most important, the most precious, the most practical items were saved or displayed. Kate had had thirteen children and her husband was a drinker. This was the house of a woman who'd held it together, who'd done what had to be done, and who'd maintained her dignity.

She brought me a glass of syrupy iced tea.

"Are you stayin'?" she asked, and Clark said, "Yes."

Our room had a handmade pine double bed that was covered with three quilts.

"She made them," Clark said. "She's made quilts for her grandchildren. Every one, and there must be dozens of us. I have cousins I don't even know."

In the morning when I went into the kitchen, Kate was making coffee.

"No sugar, please," I said. She looked me over.

"You're too skinny," she said. "You'd better least put sugar on them tomatoes."

On the kitchen table were platters of scrambled eggs, toast, chicken-fried steak, and tomatoes. Yellow tomatoes, sliced in thick rounds. I put one on a plate, cut it in half with a fork, and took a bite.

"It's warm!"

"Just picked it," Kate said. "Gets hot here early this time of year."

I ate all the tomatoes on the table so she picked more and I ate them, too.

"Clarky and Bobby, they had a hard life," she said. "Their pa, he beat those boys every day, never seen anything that bad, little as they were, and he'd be beatin' on them."

"Clark had a bad time in Vietnam, too," I said. "He went twice. The second time, he was a tail-gunner in a helicopter that was shot down."

"War breaks 'em," she said. "They don't come home the same."

I told her my father hadn't come home at all, and she said sometimes they don't want to.

She put a slab of chicken-fried steak on my plate.

Two weeks later, in Atlanta, Georgia, I felt different.

"I think I'm pregnant," I said.

64

We returned to Pasadena on Interstate 20 across the Deep South. It was early September, and as we left Alabama and crossed into Mississippi, the humid weight of late summer thickened, and the air blurred the heavy roadside vegetation. Signs indicated that towns, hidden by tangled vines, lay beyond the highway. Suddenly before us was Philadelphia, black letters on white wood, the starkest road sign I've ever seen.

Philadelphia, Mississippi. It had been only a decade since Goodman, Schwerner and Cheney, young men our age, had been murdered there while registering black voters during the Freedom Summer. The road sign could have been a grave marker.

Clark said we needed gas, and we took an exit at Meridian.

In Meridian, bound by our single credit card, we drove until we found a decrepit Shell station with a sign that advertised gas at 31 cents a gallon.

"Is that right?" Clark asked. The summer of 1974 was the height of the OPEC crisis, and gas had shot to 53 cents a gallon.

"You dreamin'?" the owner said. "I just don't change the sign no more."

He was old to us, probably in his early fifties. White. His khaki Shell uniform was stained with grease, his dusty face was streaked with sweat. He approached our car carefully—Teddy was sitting up majestically in the back seat—and glanced at our license plates. Clark had not yet registered the Chevelle in California; it still had Texas plates.

"Car needs a cleanin'," he said. "I'll get my boy."

He shouted and a black man with gray hair walked out of the garage office with some soiled rags and a spray bottle. He avoided eye contact with both of us.

"Get your missus out of the car," the owner said to Clark. To me, he said, "You need a Coke?"

I was thirsty but I didn't want a Coke. Do you have anything else I said, and he said he had all kinds of Coke: grape, strawberry, lime, root beer.

"Oh," I said, "Coke is generic for soda?"

"How much is the car wash?" Clark asked quickly. "Can we put it on the Shell card?"

"Cash," the owner said. "You can give the boy whatever you want. Two bits."

The "boy" had hand-scrubbed outside and thoroughly cleaned in the front seat, even though guarded by Teddy.

We camped off the road in a clearing in the woods outside of Shreveport, Louisiana. The tail end of a tropical storm huffed and puffed against the sides of the tent and the kerosene lanterns flickered and swayed. We sat up all night and played cards.

In the morning, we counted our money. We had $3.40, enough for two breakfasts.

After we ate, Clark made a collect call to Tulsa. Bob agreed to wire us enough money to get back to Pasadena.

"Will seventy-five bucks do it?" he asked, and Clark said yes, that would be enough.

It was.

In May, when our son Maximilian was born, a package arrived from Indiana. Inside was a handmade baby-blue-and-red quilt and a card with a stork that said *Congratulations!* Inside, under the printed greeting, was written only *Kate*.

There may have been medical reasons for my inability to ever conceive again. And yet...never again did I have a breakfast of yellow tomatoes, sliced and sugared and warm from the morning sun.

On the eleventh floor

A division of Dun & Bradstreet with offices on Fifth Avenue acquired *Datamation* in 1979 and I moved to New York with four-year-old Max and without Clark.

Two years later, I left the computer industry to become the editor of "the magazine for executive women," *Savvy*. The work was challenging and glamorous. I was on "Oprah!" when she was syndicated in only five states; I had lunch with Jane Pauley; I was interviewed by Bryant Gumbel on *Today* and David Hartman on *Good Morning, America*. I was a guest on the McLaughlin Group, and made several appearances—as an expert on women in the workplace—on *Sally Jessy Raphael*. I gave speeches to women's groups across the country, places to which I flew first class. Limousines and private drivers met my flights. I was invited to attend a four-day product announcement for mousse—*hair* mousse—in London, and Max was included in the invitation. Baskets of swag delivered to *Savvy*'s offices were so abundant and so frequent that when I finally left the job, I was stunned to realize I hadn't paid for a bottle of shampoo in five years.

I quit my position as editor of *Savvy* for two reasons. One was that I had begun to believe the entrepreneurial mantra we published: if you have a dream and work hard enough you'll succeed. The second reason was that one night, when I landed at La Guardia at 10 p.m. on a flight from a speech in Pittsburgh, my chauffeur wasn't there. I had no idea how to get home, to upper Westchester County, without a driver. I screamed into the phone at my assistant, who'd been asleep in her apartment in Brooklyn. I took a cab—a regular cab!—into Manhattan and checked into the Carlyle.

The next morning, as I replayed the drama of the night before, I had a flashback to the end of my marriage to Dan nearly twenty years earlier.

I'm not suffering, I thought. I'm just making other people suffer.

Six weeks later, with no visible or invisible means of support, I resigned from *Savvy*, and rented an office on the eleventh floor of an unfashionable building in the "Indian neighborhood" of South Park Avenue.

The eleventh floor had a demarcation line between the businesses that represented new attempts at gentrification (a law firm and an ad agency), and the smaller businesses, one of which was mine, that were old-school: a mom-and-pop manufacturer of men's polyester ties; an accountant; and me, a one-person book publishing company.

The accountant, Herb, was an Orthodox Jew; his assistant, Beverly, was Reform.

"Herb was Reform, too," Bev told me, "before he got all religious after his mother died. Don't ask. But next door," she waved toward the tie business, "even though he doesn't have the *peyots* or wear the black clothes, they're Hasidim. He can't look or speak to other women, except his wife and daughters. And his employees. Not even to say hello." I had noticed this from the small man who walked quickly to the bathroom from his factory with his head down. If we occasionally met in the hall, he averted his eyes. His wife, however, had nodded to me a few times. I had been hoping she and I could chat more. I was lonely up there on the eleventh floor running a failing business by myself.

The Tie People employed four or five South American seamstresses, all of whom, for the convenience of the management, were Seventh-Day Adventists. Everyone honored the same Sabbath.

I moved into the building in July. As fall approached, the days became shorter, and the tie factory closed earlier and earlier on Fridays.

In mid-September, the Tie Woman knocked on my open door.

"Hello," she said. "You're not Jewish, are you?"

I said no, I was a Methodist.

"Good," she said. "That's good. You will stay here on Friday nights and wait for the UPS pickup. Yes?"

And so, for four years, that's what I did. On Fridays, the Tie People and their seamstresses closed up shop an hour before sundown and I went home on the 7:10 train.

"They've got a name for what you are," the UPS driver said. "You're some kind of guy."

I asked Bev. "You're the *shabbas goy*," she said. "The non-Jew who stays late on the Sabbath to see that the work is finished."

Once I had a purpose, I became part of the eleventh floor family. Lillian the Tie Woman came by to visit every day. Sometimes her daughters and grandchildren—in my memories, they all have thick, curly, dark red hair—came with her.

There were many children, more each year, and they landed on the eleventh floor in a cloud of excitement, rushing from the elevator, shouting "Zeide! Zeide!" for their grandfather.

Lillian and I talked of children and husbands and families. She had been born in Belgium, and she'd had a younger brother. When they were three and six years old, their parents took them to a convent and gave them to the nuns to hide until the war was over. Lillian never saw her parents again. She and her brother lived with the nuns for five years. During that time, they were taught their own religious traditions, and they were taught the rituals of Mass.

"The SS would come to Mass," Lillian said, "and watch to see if there were any children who didn't know how to make the sign of the cross, who didn't know the prayers.

69

That's how much they wanted to find us, those men, us tiny children."

The convent school was across a small park from the living quarters.

"The nuns hung a painting of Jesus on the back door of the house that faced the park," Lillian said. "They told us, you must stop in the woods of the park every day and look for the face of Jesus. If you see him, come home. If you do not see him, if the picture is turned around, stay in the park for as long as you have to, until you can see him again. If the face of Jesus is hidden, that means the soldiers are here."

Lillian and her brother spent many nights crouched under shrubs, wet and cold.

"But safe," she said. "We were safe."

Her husband began to nod at me when he passed the door or met me in the hallway.

One day, I said, "Hello, Zeide," and he smiled.

The next day, he said hello.

"Zeide speaks to me," I told Bev.

"Zeide!? Why do you call him Zeide?," she said. "Don't you know that means 'grandfather'? His real name is Irving."

"Is Irving Belgian, too?" I asked Lillian.

"Irving? Who told you Irving? That's only for business. His name is Tevya."

Tevya wasn't Belgian, he was Hungarian. He, with his father and mother and sister, were gathered up from their village in the last days of the war and transported to Auschwitz. When the train arrived, the women were separated from the men and sent to the gas ovens.

In the spring of 1945, a few days before V-E day, Tevya's father died in his arms. When the Americans liberated the camp, Tevya, who was 18, weighed 68 pounds. He spent nearly a year recovering in a military hospital before he was able to emigrate to the U.S., where the government had helped him locate a cousin.

Lillian and Tevya, who had operated their tie company on the eleventh floor for more than 30 years, decided to move their business to Brooklyn. On their final day, Lillian came in to tell me that she had left more than 100 bolts of cloth in the factory, and that I was welcome to them, and to anything else they were leaving behind.

I went across the hall with her and carried a few of the bolts of polyester and wool fabric back to my office. What really took my fancy, however, was a wooden, mirrored medicine cabinet.

"That old thing?"

Lillian laughed. Tevya removed it from the wall with a crowbar.

"I am sad to leave you," Lillian said. "You are my only non-Jewish friend."

"And you," I said, "are my only friend from Brooklyn."

A few minutes before they locked their door and left, Tevya came into my office.

"I want to wish you well in all that you do," he said. I stood up, walked around to the front of my desk and held out my hand. Shaking hands with a woman is not allowed; still, it seemed like the right thing to do.

Instead, Tevya put his hands on my shoulders.

"You have been our good friend," he said. "Thank you."

I kept meaning to go see them, to call, to write, but I wasn't sure quite how to do it. What if I came at the wrong time, or said something wrong, and how do you get to Brooklyn, anyway.

I made a quilt from the material they left me, and the medicine cabinet hangs in our guest room. When I see it, I know I'm safe.

JOE PAUL

When people ask me how many times I've been married, I say, "Four times in the eyes of the state and six times in the eyes of God."

I'm neither proud nor ashamed of the count. The list includes my marriage to Dan, a legal marriage that today would not be a divorce, it would be a live-in boyfriend breakup; a legal marriage to Clark; and a live-in with Ewing, 15 years that was a marriage. Along the way, there was James and his children, a family live-in that felt like a marriage; and a brief (we lived together four nonconsecutive months) legal marriage, when I was in my early fifties, to someone who, it turned out, was not quite ready to be unmarried to his former wife.

My recovery from that final twilight zone took years, two of which I spent seeing a shrink, who may have been a nun. Whether she was or not, she fixed what she could, and gave me a toolbox to carry with me so I could do tune-ups on my own.

I slowly began dating pleasant, normal men, most of whom I met through newspaper ads in the Portland *Oregonian*. In late 1998, I ventured into the world of Yahoo Personals—a prehistoric version of online dating—and, after placing a notice that netted dozens of interesting, appropriate prospects, John Lestina and I met, per plan, at the top of the escalator at the airport in San Juan, Costa Rica.

We had written over 50 emails, talked for a thousand dollars' worth of telephone calls, and exchanged photographs. (In the early era of Internet romances, there were no photographs, unless one was requested. John had told me that he shaved his head, that he was completely bald. Nevertheless, it was a bit unnerving when his photo arrived in my email. My internet connection was dial-up, and it took nearly two minutes for the photo to scroll down. One full minute of that scroll was only top-of-head and forehead.)

I told Max I'd met a man on the Internet and that he'd sent me a ticket to join him in Costa Rica.

"You know I love you and I want you to be happy, right?" Max said. "You're coming back in a suitcase."

At the time, I was living in Oregon. My "brief, unfortunate marriage," as the divorce attorney called it, had taken me to Portland. Max was a senior at Oregon State in Corvallis. One weekend while I was visiting him I had an epiphany that Corvallis would be a good place to live. (I couldn't return to Ferndale for two reasons. One, I had house-sitters at the ranch and I was reluctant to evict them; and two, I was ashamed to return to Ferndale after another failed marriage.)

I rented a cottage across the street from the Oregon State campus.

Max was not happy.

"People are saying, 'Hey, Max, how was your summer?' and I say, 'My mother just moved here,' and they say, 'Oh, man, bummer.'"

One day as I was grocery shopping at Fred Meyer, I walked around the cereal aisle and bumped into Max buying ski gloves.

"This is exactly what I was afraid would happen!" he said. "Don't stop and talk! Just keep shopping!"

After a week on a coffee plantation guest house in Costa Rica, John drove from his home on the Midwestern plains to

74

Corvallis, packed the contents of my cottage into a trailer, and took me back to Bricelyn, Minnesota, population 400.

Bricelyn is situated six miles south of I-90, on the Iowa border, and is surrounded by thousands of acres of corn and soybeans. The only place I could buy fresh lettuce was in Albert Lea, 25 miles to the northeast.

John's house had been built for a pharmacist in the 1930s when the town was prospering and the farmlands were owned by families whose children went to the town's schools. John bought his house after corporate agricultural had taken over. As the family farms folded or sold out, so did the families. The schools closed. The Main Street businesses failed. John paid $6,500 for a three-story, gracious brick home on a third of an acre.

We drove into the driveway in the dark and left the unpacking for morning.

We were still sleeping at 6:30, when I heard the front door bang open (there were no locks in Bricelyn: only one person "took things" and if you were missing something, you went over to his house and got it back).

A deep baritone yelled, "Jooooooohn!"

I listened and could determine from upstairs that heavy footsteps were continuing into the kitchen.

"John!" I said. "Someone's here!"

He leapt out of bed.

"I didn't realize it was this late!" he said.

Our house, as I soon learned, was the men's morning hangout in Bricelyn. For nearly six years, John had lived there alone, unfettered by convention, free to be his easy-going, entertaining, *mi casa es su casa* self.

The baritone voice belonged to our next-door neighbor, Joe Paul, who was already making coffee in what was to be my kitchen and was already dropping cigarette ashes on what was to be my kitchen counter.

I dressed quickly and went downstairs.

Sitting on the circular leatherette bench that curved around the kitchen table was a man with a huge, undisciplined body that, when erect, filled up six-feet-four-inches of vertical space. A profuse amount of black hair fell over his head, his face, and much of his ornately tattoo'd skin.

Joe Paul was polite. He welcomed me, not to Bricelyn or the neighborhood, but, to my discomfort, to the house.

We talked for five or six minutes before he said something inappropriate.

I was 55. I had no intention of tolerating boorish friends of a new boyfriend.

"Don't ever talk like that in this house," I said. "It is offensive and boring."

"Okay," he said.

And with only a few lapses, he kept his word, which was quite remarkable, considering how often I saw him.

Joe Paul was in and out of our house at all hours, borrowing things, rarely returning them (John went next door when he needed one of his tools, even before he even looked in our garage). Joe Paul would arrive with news or, when it looked like we had company, to gather news.

John wanted a church wedding. I flinched. This was my fourth wedding, although none had been in a church. Still, I wanted to please John, who was marrying only for the second time legally or the third time in the eyes of God.

My plan was for something small, miniscule. Low-key to the point of no-key.

John has two grown sons, Mike and Gregg. They live in New Jersey.

"I want my boys to come," John said, and I said, "I want Max here, too."

"The Fourth of July is Bricelyn's centennial," Joe Paul said, because how could we discuss our wedding without Joe Paul. "There's gonna be fireworks, a big parade. That's when to have a wedding."

What could be more low-key? I said fine, and Joe Paul said, "I'm in charge of the pig."

The pig became the centerpiece of our planning: the ordering of the pig, the interviewing of the pig farmers to

76

determine who had the best price, driving to Blue Earth to buy the pig, how much of the pig was Joe Paul's wedding present and how much we owed him and what about the gas to Blue Earth? It evolved into an all-day, all-night roasting of the pig outside in the space between our houses, by the lovely lawn and gardens I had prepared for the Victorianesque finger-food reception. The centerpiece of our yard became the huge, stained fraternity-house overstuffed torn sofas that Joe Paul dragged out from his garage so he and his buddies—did I mention the Harleys yet?—could rest while the pig roasted.

In the meantime, bits and pieces of information about my new romance had trickled back to California.

Sara called Giuliana.

"How are you guys getting to Wendy's wedding?" she asked, and Giuliana said, "We weren't invited."

"I wasn't either," said Sara, "but I'm going. We can't let her marry someone we don't know out in the middle of the prairie."

Sue had already sent me an email that said, "I'm going to be the maid of honor. You don't have any say in that."

Sara persuaded another Pasadena-era friend, Linda Lewis, to come as well. The five Californians booked rooms at the Super8 in Albert Lea. They took over the plans for the reception and cooked from the moment they walked into the house. John's childhood friends from Minneapolis came down and his buddy Jack came two days' early with the essentials of an open bar.

John's sister, Trudy, and her husband, Bill, and her ex-husband, Chuck, and his girlfriend, Alice were there, as was my college roommate who now lived in St. Paul.

Max made it, too, barely. He was scheduled to travel from the Minneapolis airport with Sue. Her plane was landing a few minutes after his and she was renting a car.

He decided to kill those few minutes in the airport bar. He never heard her several pages. Sue waited an hour, gave up, rented the car and headed for Bricelyn.

Fifteen miles south of the airport, a thunderstorm struck; she was driving in near-zero visibility. Suddenly, on the side of the road, she spotted a man with a duffel bag.

"I don't know why I pulled over," she said. "I never pick up hitchhikers."

She clicked the button to unlock the doors. The hitchhiker opened the back door, tossed the duffel bag in the back seat, shut the door, opened the front passenger door and jumped in.

"Thanks, man," he said, and Sue said, "I don't think this is funny, Max."

It was 101 degrees on the Fourth of July in 1999 in Bricelyn, Minnesota. Neither John nor I remember that—we know from the pictures of his sons and his best man in soaked shirts.

We were married by a woman, a Methodist minister from another town, in a tiny, century-old and long-closed Baptist church that Bricelyn was renovating into a museum. John's sons, Mike and Gregg, tenor and bass, sang "Morning Has Broken," and Max gave me away.

The reception was at the senior center two blocks from the church. We were driven there in a carefully restored Model T, the ride a surprise present from local friends. It was pristine and classy—and that moment lasted only a few seconds before we were surrounded by a phalanx of roaring Harleys.

I gave my new husband The Look.

He shrugged. "Joe Paul's idea."

My friends enjoyed the wedding and they enjoyed Minnesota. In the two days before the ceremony, they attended the Miss Bricelyn contest, set up an elaborate bocce court in our yard, planned and executed the food and decorations for the reception. Giuli and Sandy visited the Jolly Green Giant statue in Blue Earth. Linda Lewis toured the farm roads on the back of Joe Paul's motorcycle

The initial two years of our marriage, as John and I traveled back and forth between Bricelyn and Ferndale, Joe Paul "watched" our house. Joe Paul had a very nice yellow farmhouse of his own, and a smart but understandably impatient wife.

For Joe Paul, watching our house was an answer to prayer. We'd return to a television set still holding a forgotten XXX video, garbage bags of beer cans in the basement, ashtrays filled with roaches, and odd bits of clothing from unknown characters who'd needed a place to crash for a night or two. More than once in those years I'd meet someone new, and he'd say, "Oh, I know where you live. It's Joe Paul's other house."

Nevertheless, after hundreds of hours of cooking and cleaning while Joe Paul sat at my kitchen table and spun his theories of life and love and motorcycle maintenance, I found I missed him if a few days went by without him crashing through the front door and yelling. He was thoughtful, he stood up well during endless debates, and he was kind.

One Sunday morning, five years after we moved to Ferndale, Joe Paul—in his own house, in his own kitchen—had a heart attack and died. He was 52.

FRANK IS COVERED

Until John and I turned 65 and became eligible for Medicare, we were not insured. We did not have employers who offered us insurance and we could not afford private health insurance.

Twice a year we went across the river to Christ Lutheran Church in Fortuna, where the Humboldt County Health Department held a Senior Health Day in the Sunday school rooms. A public health nurse spent more than an hour with us, individually, discussing every aspect of our lives and determining how we could prevent illness and improve our safety without spending very much money.

It was an outstanding program, funded by the state. Just before I qualified for Medicare—after the crash of the housing market and the subsequent bankruptcies and foreclosures took a toll on state tax revenue—the program was eliminated. We tossed the dice for a while longer, remained healthy, and crossed safely into federal insurance land.

Until that happy day, John and I were the only ones in our household who were uninsured. Our dog, Frank, whom we acquired from the county pound when he was an adult dog with two prior placements, had an excellent policy.

Frank's policy was free for the first three months; after that, we paid a monthly premium of nine dollars.

As soon as we returned home from the pound with Frank, I called ShelterCare, his insurance company, and registered him.

"He is a McNab/Australian shepherd mix, he's neutered, he's two, and he's had his shots."

When the form was completed, the customer service representative said, "Perhaps you have other animal companions who may need health coverage?"

I said we had a crippled, aging German shepherd; one cat; eight chickens; and three boarding horses, average age 26.

"We have an excellent indoor cat plan," she said.

"She's not an indoor cat," I said. "Coyotes already ate Simone, our Siamese."

"We have death benefits," she said.

I felt a good idea coming on.

As Doc Detlefsen was a veterinarian, I know that veterinary medicine, in many respects, does not differ much from Homo sapiens medicine. And even if it did, by now I would be immune to the differences. During my childhood, Doc came home with medicine and my mother the nurse administered it to us, the neighbors, and anyone else in town who self-diagnosed "the flu" and was willing to drive down the alley and come up the side steps to the kitchen, where glass syringes boiled noisily in Revere Ware saucepans on the electric stove.

We were shot with veterinary streptomycin or whatever other antibiotic was in style and we survived.

I was never sick. I went years in elementary school without an absence and would have had the same record in high school if I'd finished book reports on time.

After reading the promotional literature on ShelterCare, I called Kevin Silver at Ferndale Veterinary. My plan was to register myself as, say, Kittykins, an eight-and-a-half-year-old—my age in cat years—and receive medical insurance.

Top-drawer medical insurance. ShelterCare is not some Blue-Crossy limited deal. Frank was covered for X-rays, prescriptions, surgeries, hospitalization, ultrasounds,

MRI/CAT scans, homeopathic treatments including acupuncture and chiropractic, chemo, and referrals. Frank could select the veterinarian of his choice. His coverage accepted conditions of heredity and congenital defects, even the dreaded hip dysplasia. All breeds of dogs and cats in the world were eligible except Shar Peis, which, the ShelterCare customer service rep said, have been inbred to the point of becoming an unacceptable insurance risk.

"If you have a Shar Pei who isn't sick," she said, "you have a miracle."

I was impressed to hear that the indoor cat policy honored claims of up to $1,200 in cases of poisoning.

This would have been valuable to us in 2000 when my parents poisoned me.

It was probably an accident.

John and I stopped by my mother's house on our way to in Eureka. It was about 10 in the morning, and I had a headache. I never have headaches.

My mother was playing solitaire on her computer. Without looking up, she reached for a bottle of Bayer baby aspirin out of a drawer and told me to take two.

I shook them out in my hand. They were larger than I had remembered baby aspirin, and they were white. Max's baby aspirins had been pink. But babies are bigger now and white is probably a gender-blind color. I popped two and left.

Somewhere in the Costco aisles between the wine and the popcorn poppers, my mind left for Saturn and my body quickly followed.

"I'm. Sick."

John suggested I needed something to eat. By the time we were seated I was unable to keep my upper body erect.

"Call. Mom. Now."

"Oh, dear," she said. "Daddy says that wasn't baby aspirin. He says that was his morphine. He hid it there so…*other people*…wouldn't find it."

She told me to go home and sleep it off.

Three hours later I struggled to the phone and called Tom Renner, the town pharmacist.

"Isn't there some kind of reverse-overdose pill I can take?" I said, and Tom said, "Doc's dosage is in 50-milligram pills. You've ingested 100 milligrams of morphine, and you have no receptors. Get to the emergency room. Now. We don't even have time to call an ambulance. Tell John to shove you in the car and drive as fast as he can to Redwood Memorial. Your respiratory system is shutting down. I'll call them and tell them to be ready for you."

It was too late for stomach-pumping. I got the junkie shot. I didn't feel a thing. John watched and he said the needle looked like something that would be used on a horse.

The withdrawal took 72 hours, my entire weekend, and the worst was yet to come—a $600 charge from the hospital.

I asked the poisoners if they would pay for part of it.

"Don't be ridiculous," my mother said. "You should know better than to take other people's medications."

"Maybe I'll file charges of attempted murder," I said, and she said, "That's a good one."

Under ShelterCare, all costs would have been covered.

Other than committing fraud, I could see no downside to the Kittykins plan.

"Are there drawbacks?" I asked Kevin Silver.

"If you were to stay over following surgery," he said, "you might find the accommodations a bit spare. We give you a pad and a big blankie but you would be lying on cement, with no TV, no adjustable bed. You'd be in a private room, though—we only have private rooms. And I don't think the food would be that much different from hospital food."

"What about medications? Aren't we all taking more or less the same stuff?"

"For small injuries, little wounds, the treatment would be the same. And antibiotics are more or less equal, although the delivery systems, the inert stuff that carries the antibiotics into the system, are not all the same. Human penicillin is packed in corn starch, for example. It would be different, say, for a dog. Blood work would be the same, though. All our blood chemistry work is done in the labs at St. Joseph's. Runs on the same machines."

"There is no way to tell animal blood from human blood?"

"Not unless you're a goat, a camel, or a bird. Bird blood has a nucleus, and camel blood cells—goats are related to that family—are oval. Animals have more blood types than humans. And they're compatible, for the most part. When we do a transfusion on a dog, for example, especially a first-time transfusion, we just bring in a big dog for the donor. The blood types don't have to match."

I mentioned the cost savings and Kevin said yes, I would save money in Ferndale, but in larger, specialized animal clinics down below, I could expect to pay much more for such procedures as hip replacement, eye surgeries, and kidney transplants.

"Animals are getting organ transplants?"

"Oh, yes. A few weeks ago, I even did a complete work-up on a hamster. I've operated on quite a few pet rats, removing tumors, taking care of illnesses."

"*Rats* are getting better medical care than I am?"

"Yes, well, that seems to be the case," Kevin said. "Do I detect a tone of righteous indignation?"

Later, I calmed down. I was off-track in my conversation with Kevin. Rats are not eligible for medical insurance. They're full-pay patients. Like us.

STAR OF THE WEEK

It was an early Sunday afternoon in late January, the light slowly changing from a bright taupe to a moldy gray. Ten minutes of raucous, televised professional football had exhausted us. We were preparing for a nap when Frank gave a hello "Woof."

"Wendy!" Tony Valverde pushed the front door open. "I'm Star of the Week!"

He walked in carrying a fat green folder and a small stuffed animal. Tony had just completed half of his kindergarten year at Ferndale Elementary School.

Star of the Week, he explained, granted quite a few honors, including custodial care of Benny, an eight-inch brown bear in a red-and-white striped nightcap.

Rosa, Tony's mother, followed him into the house.

"Tony's here for all day," she said. "He has homework."

She handed me a memo the kindergarten teachers, Diane and Heather, had written in English to the parents.

"Thank you, Wendy," she said, and left.

John and I are the American parents and grandparents to the Valverdes, a Mexican family from the central highlands of the state of Oaxaca. They adopted us.

It began simply enough. Rosa and Antonio and their son, Tony, three years old, lived in a trailer on a knoll where, 80 years ago, a creamery processed milk from 30 nearby family dairies. Antonio's *padrone* was third-generation from one of those families.

The shelter provided to Antonio and Rosa, a "trailer," was not the type of trailer that auto-corrects to "mobile home." Their shelter defaulted to "used camper." It wasn't large enough to house either an indoor toilet or a refrigerator. A rough shed behind the used camper housed a toilet that had no discernible connection to a sewage system, and an avocado green refrigerator, a cast-off from 1972, stood in the front yard, charged with electricity from a pole via an orange industrial extension cord.

Every day I drove into town on Centerville Road, and every day when I passed the knoll with the camper on it I wondered if that family needed help.

I was not quick to act, however, and it wasn't from awkwardness. It was because I knew what not to do. On Thanksgiving of 1971 I had prepared a feast of turkey and dressing and cornbread and sweet potato pie and mashed potatoes and cranberry sauce, and James and the children and Grandma and Uncle Harold and I were ready to eat when there was a knock on the door. Two pretty high school girls from San Marino, one whose father was the president of the Pacific Coast Stock Exchange, were standing on the porch of my house holding a box of food. Whatever and whoever I thought I was before I opened that door, I learned in that instant I wasn't.

Therefore, when it came to the family on the knoll, I knew what not to do: knock on their door with a huge box of food. I had no alternative plan so I did nothing.

I did nothing, but I did pray, not like people pray out loud in church or on television, but how people pray when they just want to get a few things straight. *Okay, God, here's the thing, look at how hard this man works and how crappy his house is. What am I supposed to do about it? Nothing? If it's nothing, what's the point of this worrying? If it's something, give me a clue. A big clue. Okay?*

Months passed. Summer rolled around, and with it came ridiculously abundant crops of Yukon gold potatoes and tomatillos.

One afternoon I was driving home from town and the mother from the knoll was walking alongside the road with her little boy, who was riding a tricycle.

I stopped in the middle of the road, rolled down the window, and said, "Hola!"

For years I had been underemployed often enough to have had the time to teach myself an elementary level of Spanish that left me fluent enough to ask if she liked potatoes and tomatillos. As a self-teaching language instructor, I favor nouns over conjugated verbs. My conversations relay objects and people and a vague reference to action, but have no nuance, no framework of time and motion.

I didn't think this mattered until I tried out my new skills on Giuliana.

"I am so impressed, my friend, that you are speaking Spanish," she said. "Soon, maybe you will want to take formal lessons."

"Why? Everyone understands me."

"Yes, but someday you might want to say something more advanced than 'I go Fortuna.'"

Maybe. But that afternoon, alongside Centerville Road, when I told Rosa where I lived and invited her to come over and help us dig potatoes and pick tomatillos, she said, "Okay!" and within an hour she and her son Tony were at our house.

John and Rosa packed the vegetables into cardboard boxes while Tony and I sat on the deck and ate ice cream. Rosa joined us and we talked until we both knew everything—men and families, births and deaths and love— that was necessary for us to be friends.

That's about it. Within a year, we had 46 people, all members of *la familia*, on our Christmas list. And we were on theirs. After Christmas our house was decorated with mirrors painted with landscapes of Fiji and sound tracks of warbling cuckoos; flying dolphins in golden frames; the baby Jesus in a manger with iridescent fiber-optic hay; and a mirror decorated with a painting of the adult Jesus whose bleeding heart was superimposed on psychedelic starbursts that were strobe lights. The piles of antique, handmade quilts on our bed were gone and a red satin bedspread centered with a queen-sized valentine flanked by outsized roses had taken their place.

"Wow!" I had said when I unwrapped the package.

Rosa was matter-of-fact about replacing the quilts.

"It's bad luck to have rags on the marriage bed," she said.

The Star of the Week had three tasks. Write a report on what activities he did with Benny. Draw a picture of Benny. Write an autobiography based on a list of provided questions.

"Where are my colors?" Tony asked. I explained that the long winter of remodeling had displaced everything in the house, and that if I couldn't find my toothbrush it was doubtful his crayons were accessible.

"I'll look upstairs!" he said, racing up to the loft. "Here they are!"

Benny the Bear slumped against a pile of books and posed for the portrait.

"I'm just going to lie down for a minute while you color," I said, and Tony said, "I'm finished!"

"Quite a good likeness," I said.

The three of us curled up in the pink-peony-upholstered overstuffed chair for story-writing time.

"You hold Benny," Tony said, and when I did a scrap of white paper uncurled from the back of his tee-shirt.

"What's this?"

"These are his papers," I said. "They say where Benny is from."

We read the label.

"Benny is from China!"

Tony was excited. We'd talked about China often, conversations sparked by its name on the sides of his tennis shoes.

This revelation about Benny's origins made the assignment much easier. Whereas the most recent Star of the Week had written that she took Benny on a bicycle ride to her aunt's house, Tony wrote, or rather, dictated, how he had taken Benny on a helicopter ride to visit family in China, where he had played basketball. Benny had returned to Ferndale on a boat that was briefly overturned by a sea dragon.

Only the questionnaire remained. Name, easy. Where do you live?

"Fortuna?"

I explained, no, Fortuna is across the river, over the bridge. We live in Ferndale. He was confused. Ferndale is the town. It's where the school is, where most of the houses are, where the stores are.

"Yes," I said, "but Ferndale is also the country around the town." I dodged the temptation to explain county government and city limits. We tackled question number three.

"Who are the people in your family?"

We breezed through "what my family does for fun"—"Laugh with my dad"—and came to the question about his future.

"When I grow up I want to be…" Here there was no hesitation.

"A man!" he said.

I've known more than a few louts who would have been well served to have focused on this life goal, but I made the dull, adult mistake of leading Tony back into Formland. No, I said, this question is asking what kind of work you want to do when you are a man. Tony responded with far less enthusiasm.

"Computers."

That's how fast a sea-monster-scrapping adventurer can be reduced to a tax code.

Time for toast.

In my mailbox, my neighbor Linda had left a gift, a jar of orange-whipped honey from the Cistercian Sisters at the

Redwood Monastery. The honey flowed nicely into the holes of John's homemade bread.

The snack changed our conversation, honey leading, as Winnie-the-Pooh so often noted, to the subject of bees.

"After they suck it up from the flowers," Tony said, "what do they do with it?"

"Vomit," I said, "back in their waxy little house."

"Cool," Tony said.

Re-engaged with the tasks for the Star of the Week, we moved through the easy questions about favorite toys and favorite food, and then, another stumper.

"Where does your family go for vacation?"

Immigrants who milk cows twice a day don't take vacations. The Eel River Valley was founded on that reality, from the Irish and French Canadians to the Danes, the Swiss, the Italians, the Portuguese, and now the Mexicans, each successive migration employed by the former to work night and day.

"When your dad doesn't have to work," I said. "And you go somewhere in the car, where do you go?"

"To the snow!" he said. That would be five miles south of town, up the Wildcat road and into the hills that overlook the ocean. Snow, rare along the northern California coastline, sticks up there long enough to throw a few snowballs.

Next question.

"I have a collection of—"

"What's a c'lection?"

"A collection is a bunch of things you have that are all the same. See those sugar bowls on the shelf over the fireplace? Let's count them. One, two...six. That's a collection. Three or more things that are the same."

"Why?"

"Why what?"

"Why do you want more than one?"

"Because...because we like to have things around us that make us happy. When we find something that makes us happy, we get another one just like it and we get even happier."

We stopped talking.

Tony took Benny out of my arms and looked into the bear's face. Benny gazed back, his mouth in a wistful twist.

I was congratulating myself on my brilliant—really, there is no other adjective as apt—my brilliant explanation. I should have been a teacher. I have a natural gift for communicating with children. Extraordinary, how I was able to define a complex concept, and to a bicultural child—

"Wendy! I know what I collect!"

He was smiling with his entire face, his cheeks forced apart, his full set of baby teeth exposed. Benny had cheered up as well.

"Love!" Tony shouted. "I collect love!"

There is no more to this story.

There never has been and there never will be.

JEANNE

My grandmother, Minna Emma Boese, was born in 1872 into a German family living on a farm near a German village in the Ukraine. The Germans had been invited to Russia by Catherine the Great who admired their agricultural skills; the lure had been free land, no taxes, and no forced military service. The food-production plan was a big success. The social plan was a disaster. People who already lived in the Ukraine, who had to pay for land, pay taxes, and serve in the military, were not inclined to welcome the privileged immigrants who lived well, and unassimilated, in the separate villages. Every so often a German settlement would be burned and its occupants driven out or killed, a practice that continued without any governmental intervention for a couple of centuries. Eventually my ancestors tired of the persecution, and in 1886, when Minna was 14, she escaped with her father, her stepmother and her crippled half-brother Harry. (This is something I don't understand. If someone doesn't want you in their country, to the point of killing you in your own town, why do they also want to kill you if you try to leave?)

Minna's sister Johanna and a brother were captured and sent to work camps in Siberia. The fate of the brother was never certain. Johanna survived for decades. My mother, who was born in 1914, remembers her parents filling boxes with packaged food, clothing, and tools "for Johanna" and mailing them to Russia.

The Boese family immigrated to America and settled in Cathay, a small German town in North Dakota. Five years later, when Minna was 19, she married Maximilian Ferdinand Folendorf, so-named because his half-French mother was enamored with the ill-fated Emperor of Mexico.

A year later Minna gave birth to a son, the first of what were to be eight children over a period of 24 years. My mother, Maxine, the seventh child, had nieces and nephews who were her contemporaries.

Jeanne, the eighth child, was born when Minna was 45. Jeanne was sickly. The doctors told Max and Minna that she would not live past the age of 10.

Her birth certificate says "Jean," just as my mother's birth certificate says "Maxine Janet." These names were not exotic enough for my mother. When she was an adolescent, she arbitrarily and permanently, not legally, changed both of their names. Jean became Jeanne (pronounced "Jeannie") Bobette, and Janet became Jenet, with a silent "t."

"Whose idea was it to call you 'Ja-neigh'?" I asked my mother once we were both in the elderly category and more truths could be told.

"Mine," she said. "It was a mistake. I wanted to be Jeanette, but I didn't spell it right. When a teacher questioned me about it, I got embarrassed so I said it was French and that it was 'Ja-neigh.'"

"And Bobette?"

"Isn't that silly!" she laughed. "Kids have such funny ideas."

She is clever that way, my mother. Even at 102, she is able to switch the subject deftly into the third person.

Shortly after I inherited the ranch, I was walking through the back bedroom where the walls were filled with framed photographs. I stopped at one to reminisce. It was a group photo taken in 1952, at Minna's 80th birthday party. In the picture my grandmother (whom we, inexplicably, called "Dona," a Spanish term for grandmother) is surrounded by her seven living children (her second child, Florence, died in 1922 of an infection due to a miscarriage).

Everyone looks happy, even Dona, who may or may not have been a happy person. I never knew her well. Soon after that birthday she had a stroke and until her death eight years later, she said only "Yes, yes" and "There, there."

In the photo my mother is laughing. The picture is black-and-white but I can still recall the vivid primary colors of her striped taffeta skirt. Jeanne, in 1952 already 25 years beyond her grim medical prognosis, is laughing, too. I peered closely and saw her familiar face as if for the first time: the slightly flat nose, the slanted eyes.

I telephoned my mother.

"Does Jeanne have Down syndrome?!"

My mother hissed.

"Don't you ever say another word about it."

I marvel now at how everything had been explained. Jeanne talked a bit funny but so do a lot of people, and she didn't have a driver's license, but that was because she was poor and couldn't afford a car, and anyway, it didn't matter because she lived in San Jose and could take the bus to work. She didn't write well, but she was good reader and that was what was important.

I had asked once if something was "wrong" with Jeanne and my mother snapped, "Of course not. She was born with a cleft palate. Happens all the time." She mentioned two Ferndale people who'd been born with cleft palates. My mother knows all the medical facts about everyone who lived in Ferndale between 1945-1949, the years she was a nurse in the doctor's office. What she has shared with me would cause HIPAA officers to turn over in their cubicles. Her explanation of what was "wrong" with Jeanne was good enough for me. I had a world of my own to think about.

Jeanne lived with Dona, who was widowed in 1936, and she worked at W. T. Grant's, a variety store. When we visited San Jose, Jeanne would come home from work with bags of cinnamon candy and stale popcorn. I wanted to have a job like hers. In later years, she became a clerk for the Rosicrucian Society in what seemed like a stretch for a devout Baptist. ("Isn't the Rosicrucian Society sort of a religion?" I asked when I visited her in the old-age home. Jeanne waved it away. "They were good people, oh, such nice people.")

Jeanne also worked at home. You may be the mother of eight, a fact that doesn't necessarily increase the odds of finding someone to take you in; fortunately, Dona had Jeanne. Jeanne was an accomplished homemaker, an excellent cook, a thorough and exacting cleaner.

And, like her mother, Jeanne was very religious. The two of them were spoken of by my mother and my aunt as a unit, Dona-and-Jeanne, and mentioned so often and with such reverence that, coupled with a tradition of giving Bibles as presents, I considered them as female stand-ins for God-and-Jesus.

Jeanne/Jesus, however, was a bit short on mercy.

"You a brat," she would say when we visited. You a brat. That's not a typo. That's the way she talked.

"A spoiled brat."

As a young woman, Jeanne's life, although free of romance, was filled with friends from her jobs and her church. Some of these friends made the mistake of underestimating her.

In the early 1950s, a married couple from her church invited Jeanne to go with them to the movies. Jeanne's jobs were basic—she stocked inventory at Grant's—and her pay was never above minimum wage. Her friends often paid for her outings.

On this particular evening the theater manager placed everyone's ticket stubs in a glass jar and held a drawing. The prize was $50 and a trip to Reno.

Jeanne's ticket was the winning number.

Everyone was happy, Jeanne for herself and the couple for her. A day or so later, perhaps after a few retellings, the generous husband and wife became less so.

They called Jeanne and claimed the right to the prize.

Jeanne may have had her challenges, but the eighth child of eight doesn't survive without being scrappy. Plus, her closest sibling was my mother, for whom the word "scrappy" was invented. (In her classic back-to-back-cliché phrasing, my mother said the two of them "fought like cats and dogs but were thicker than thieves.")

Jeanne's response to her friends' demand to relinquish the prize was a 1953 version of "I don't think so."

The couple sued her. (In small claims court? Where? I was too young to be concerned with those kinds of details, too young to ask, when I heard that Jeanne's lawyer was writing a letter, what kind of a lawyer takes a $50/bus trip to Reno case.)

There were muttered discussions between my mother and my aunt about the moral character of the so-called friends and, from my mother's point of view particularly, how could they be real Baptists, since Baptists, at least in 1953, didn't believe in lawsuits.

Jeanne won. She went to Reno with Hazel and George and if the photographic evidence is to be trusted—three smiling, dressed-up, middle-aged people sitting at a formal dining table with a centerpiece arrangement of exotic flowers—a good time was had by all.

In August 1960, at the age of 89, Dona died.

Two years later, during Whitman College's Thanksgiving break, Dan drove his car, a tiny black Datsun convertible, from snowy Walla Walla to his parents' house in Menlo Park, California. His gas was paid by the four passengers, one of whom was me. There wasn't room for four people, Dan said when I asked to ride along, adding that I would have to sit in the front on the gearshift between the bucket seats. I was thrilled. Sitting next to Dan for thirteen hours was the only reason for my trip.

"I will be spending Thanksgiving with my aunt in San Jose," I said. I may have also said that it was a family tradition, a claim that bore not even a seed of truth.

I had dated Dan five or six times, I was smitten and he was not. I was 18, I'd seen all the Doris Day movies, and I thought that if you were cute and persistent, you'd get your man. The consequences of guile were a lesson yet to be learned.

San Jose, while not far from Menlo Park, is south, and Dan wasn't willing to make the trip any longer for himself. He dropped me off at the Palo Alto bus station. I called Jeanne.

"I'm taking the bus to San Jose. I'll get a cab from there."

"That's okay," she said. "We pick you up."

"Who's 'we'? How are you getting to the station?"

"None of your beeswax."

In San Jose I was met by Jeanne and a handsome man she introduced as Jack. I was embarrassed. They were both 45 and they were holding hands.

Jack, too, had never been married. He'd worked at a union job, driving a fork lift in a Contadina tomato canning factory. Like Jeanne, he'd taken care of his widowed mother until her death a year earlier. Jeanne was his first girlfriend.

After his mother died, Jack's friends encouraged him to make some new friends, and he signed up for a church-sponsored tour of the Napa/Sonoma County wine country. On the tour bus he met Jeanne.

They began dating. One day they discovered that both sets of deceased parents were buried in the same very large cemetery. They went to visit the respective graves, parted to find the plots, walked around a corner and ran into each other. The gravesites of their parents were adjacent.

Jack and Jeanne announced their engagement at Christmas. (After I was married, my mother told me that Jack and Jeanne had visited a doctor before the wedding to ask questions about sex. Both were virgins and they wanted to know if, at 45, sex would be a problem. Reportedly, the answer is, only if you make it a problem.)

Jeanne wanted the wedding to be in Ferndale, at the ranch. In June 1963, she and Jack stood before Hazel and George's fireplace as a minister performed the ceremony.

On the half-step-flat piano, I played "You'll Never Walk Alone." Candace and Tonya and Tonya's best friend Joni sang "The Lord's Prayer" and "Always," and everyone sang "Always" and my mother and my aunt cried.

Jack and Jeanne lived happily ever after. Jack sold his house and fixed up Jeanne's house. They traveled to antique shows and the American Southwest. They bought cowboy shirts and turquoise jewelry. On Sunday mornings and Sunday nights and Wednesday nights they went to church.

They never stopped hugging and kissing and acting embarrassing for people who were so old to begin with.

Jack died in 1988. My mother went down below for the funeral.

"It was beautiful," she said. "At the end the choir sang 'Fly Me to the Moon.'"

"'Fly Me to the Moon?' Really?" I asked.

"Yes," she said. "And I want that at my funeral, too."

If my mother should predecease me, and that looks less likely all the time as she still hasn't a gray hair or an arthritic finger, I'm tempted to honor her request and have a torch singer belt out that Vegas lounge standard instead of "I'll Fly Away," the rousing gospel song which was Jack's actual sendoff.

Widowed, Jeanne lived alone in the house in San Jose.

"I am lonely," she wrote to my mother. "Remember how we sleep together like spoons when we were kids? I miss Jack every minute. I know Jesus is with us always but I wish Jesus had a real body."

When she was 90 and legally blind, Jeanne moved to a small group home for elderly women, the kind of place that appears just fine from the outside; on the inside lunch is a boxed macaroni-and-cheese, the console television doesn't work, and the furniture is clumsy, dreary and brown.

"Did Jack know that Jeanne had Down syndrome?" I asked my mother.

"I doubt it very much," she said. "No one ever said anything. I knew it all my life, of course. When we lived in

Long Beach, and I was in the third grade and Jeanne was three or four, I walked her to the doctor's office every day and they showed her how to place her tongue, how to move it to make words."

Jeanne and I didn't communicate very often until a few years ago, when she telephoned me. She had been reading *From the Back Pew*, a collection of columns I wrote at the turn of the century. When she said how much she enjoyed the stories about Ferndale, I said, "I guess you don't think I'm a brat anymore," which, not to put too fine a point on it, underscored the truth of her accusation.

Over our subsequent phone calls, Jeanne said she wanted to be with Jack, she wanted to go to church, she wanted to see her friends who had died or were too old to write to her, and she wanted Mexican food.

That we could fix. We drove down below and Google-mapped our way to the rest home with an aluminum take-out tray of chicken enchiladas.

We talked for several hours. Jeanne had not forgotten much about her life, and she told detailed, hilarious stories. We laughed. We were noisy. The Cambodian attendants gave us nervous glances. We took photographs. We hugged goodbye.

"John is wonderful, wonderful," she said, as we left. "But you still a brat."

A few months later, the telephone rang before dawn. We did not get up. We lay there, awake, not speaking, suspending the last moment in which we didn't know what news was so urgent, so raw, it couldn't wait until sunrise.

When John answered he said, "I'm sorry to hear that. But she was very unhappy where she was."

Jeanne, the child who was not expected to live past the age of 10, had died. She was 92.

My son is a father

I didn't believe my son would ever grow up.

That's not to say I was fatalistic about the infant becoming a child or the child becoming a man. As all mothers know, that transformation happens in a day. You rise before dawn: he's crying, he's hungry; you go to work, come home, and trip over a jumble of soccer equipment. You run a load of Levi's and find an unfamiliar foil wrapper in the dryer. The car engine cuts off at the top of the driveway, you check the clock. It's 3 a.m. A college acceptance surfaces at the last moment, he flunks out, goes to community college, works at Arby's to pay the tuition, graduates, moves back to New York and marries.

When Max was in junior high school, I sat across a conference table from the guidance counselor for what may have been the third or fourth time. The woman was fed up.

"Mrs. Crisp," she said, with such exasperation that each word exited her mouth as an independent heavy object. "Your. Son. Has."—she waited for the birth of lethal descriptive—"Big. Ideas."

I couldn't have been prouder.

"Big ideas!" I said. "Like Martin Luther King? Like Gandhi?"

He campaigned for president of the student body when he was a sixth-grader. His platform was the overhaul of the menu in the cafeteria and he rapped his campaign speech. I was in Albuquerque. I called home. He was frantic.

"They stomped their feet and yelled 'Max! Max! Max!'" he said. "What am I going to do if I'm elected? I didn't run to win."

"Why did you run?"

"I wanted to give the speech."

He didn't win but he came dangerously close. A few years passed without any history-making big ideas, and then, in December of his sophomore year in high school, wearing a Big Bird mask and while the orchestra was playing "Little Drummer Boy," he ran naked across the stage during the school's Christmas program.

The principal called.

"Mrs. Crisp? I have your son here in the office. He has something to tell you."

"Hi. Yeah. I guess I did something sort of stupid."

Max paused. I was silent. The range of stupidity available to a 15-year-old boy is so vast, there's no default point at which a parent can enter the narrative.

"I streaked the orchestra."

Streaking was out of fashion in 1991, and had been since about 1974, when one of Johnny Carson's writers ran naked across the stage during a live broadcast of the "Tonight" show.

"I had my escape mapped out perfectly," Max said, "but the second violins blocked the door."

I was angry. Not for the reasons the principal was about to tell me—that the district school event was attended by parents and grandparents and, most critically, young middle-school girls who may never have seen a penis—my reasons were that this was a choir and an orchestra populated by students who were overshadowed by football and cheerleading and popularity contests. This event had required training, study, and practice. This was their moment in the sun and Max had stolen it from them.

I drove Max home—he was suspended for three days—and he took to his bed.

Sometime that afternoon, he called Dr. Monkman, the Methodist pastor at the Pound Ridge Community Church.

"I've ruined my entire life," he told Dr. Monkman. "I will never be able to overcome what I've done."

Years later the pastor told me the story from his point of view.

"It was nearing Christmas, my busiest time, and I was in a meeting with the head of the church council. We were talking about church finance, and the secretary came in and said, 'Max Crisp is on the phone and I think it's an emergency.' I excused myself and took the call. He said he thought his life was over, and I told him to come in immediately.

"He sat down and I said, 'What has happened?' And he said, 'I streaked the school Christmas program.' You have to understand that we've had a lot of tragedies with young people here, runaways, drug overdoses, suicides, accidents. I was shaking before he came in, terrified of what I was about to hear. When he told me I was so relieved that, I'm sorry to confess, I laughed."

Thus exonerated by a man of the cloth, Max returned home with hope. The longer-term consequences were yet to be suffered and the short-term results were positive. He had changed his public persona in sixty seconds. Suddenly, he was popular. Eighteen months later, he was elected senior class president, an election he wanted to win, one that he had entered with a campaign to rid the school leadership of "elite, yuppie bigots." It was a Big Idea.

I had just stopped holding my breath, when one Sunday in late February of his senior year after a heavy snowfall, he and his girlfriend found a squirrel that had frozen to death.

The girlfriend, who was planning to be a veterinarian, suggested they thaw the squirrel in the microwave and dissect it.

I was only half-listening, or maybe a third-listening. Sunday was one of only two days I didn't have a five-hour-round-trip commute into Manhattan. I was slumped on the sofa watching a Woody Allen movie and doing the Sunday crossword in the *Times Magazine.*

The squirrel was disemboweled and stuffed. Sounded fine to me. A little biology lab, a little taxidermy. Those phases of the project completed, Max and Lisa removed some wooden slats off a vegetable box, asked if they could borrow a cigarette and drove off in my car.

Monday morning, the new principal of Fox Lane High School summoned me to an immediate meeting. In his office, he informed me that Max was being expelled and "obviously" would no longer be permitted to fulfill his role as senior class president.

The offense was that Lisa and Max had nailed the preserved squirrel to a makeshift cross, stuck an unlit cigarette in its mouth, and affixed the cross to a tree on private property that adjoined the school grounds—a location where students gathered every day to smoke legal and illegal substances.

The principal demanded I sign something. There were to be no explanations on our part, no hearings.

I protested. The principal said, "We happen to know this was part of a satanic rite."

I said, "I was there while this was going on. I'm not an expert on satanic rites, but I don't think they involve giggling, running in and out of my kitchen, and stopping occasionally to watch scenes from *Annie Hall.*"

"We found 666, the mark of the devil, on the slats of wood used to make the cross," the principal said.

I'd fallen through the rabbit hole. Half the students in the school came from the nearby town of Mount Kisco, where the telephone prefix is 666. He had to have known that fact.

"The wood was torn off a vegetable box in the garage," I said. "The box was from a grocery store in Mount Kisco. The number was part of the store's telephone number. I can

106

look it up —" I was talking into the wind. Mr. Kramer had no interest in facts. He was only a few months into the job, and, and he eventually made clear, he did not believe that the senior class president should be someone who, two years earlier, had streaked the Christmas program and merely had his hands slapped. Mr. Kramer emphasized that his predecessor had erred in allowing Max to continue as a Fox Lane student.

My son was two-and-a-half months away from graduation and he was toast.

From home I called Sam, our neighbor and a former chief of homicide for the Bronx who had spent his early retirement disability money on law school. Sam said he'd see what he could do.

Next, I called Charlie Lakin, the principal of Ferndale High School.

"Hello," I said, "You don't remember me probably. I'm Doc and Maxine's daughter, and Hazel and George Waldner's niece—"

"I know who you are, Wendy. What can I do for you?"

"Oh, Charlie," I cried, "they won't let my son graduate."

"An already-dead squirrel was nailed to a tree that wasn't on school property?" Charlie said after I told the story. "God, I wish I had problems like that. Send him on out, Wendy. We'll graduate him."

While our neighbor investigated our options, the injustice of the sentence spread throughout the area. Fox Lane draws its student population from several widely disparate communities, and soon kids and parents were calling, telling me something I hadn't known: two years earlier, a coach who was still in the district's employ had slugged Max in the locker room in front of an entire PE class.

The kids were willing to testify, the parents said. One mother added, "Incinerate these creeps."

In New York State the statute of limitations on an adult striking a child at school does not run out until the child is 18 and has graduated.

With this information, Sam persuaded the school board to drop the issue. His argument was brief. He documented the slugging, stated the law, referenced the witnesses, and suggested that either Max be reinstated and allowed to graduate or the district could pay us $10 million. They quickly agreed to the reinstatement but insisted that Max not be allowed to reassume the class presidency. I am sorry that Sam conceded that point; in that role, Max would have given the commencement address and would have stunningly outshone his trembling replacement.

Max's graduation took place six months after Hazel died and bequeathed me the ranch. In June, he flew to California to be a camp counselor at Cloverleaf Ranch in Santa Rosa and I bought a white 1993 Chevrolet Silverado truck, filled it with my favorite stuff, and meandered alone across America for five weeks until I arrived in Ferndale. I never looked back.

Except once. Four years later, a friend sent me a clipping from the *New York Times*. It was a story about the Fox Lane School District, and how, during the previous school year, the district had been "tied in knots" over on-campus games of Dungeons & Dragons and the accusations of two mothers that the principal—that's right! the same Foe of Lucifer!— was engaging in satanic rituals.

After months of what the *Times* reporter described as humiliating public meetings, the principal was coerced into putting the rumors to rest by standing before the crowd at a public Fox Lane School District board meeting and accepting Jesus Christ as his personal savior.

On the night of April 9, 2004, I was staying in the midtown Manhattan apartment of my friend, David Jackson. He had agreed I could sleep on his sofa for "a week or so" so I could be present for the birth of my grandchild.

At 10:30 p.m. the phone rang.

"It's time," Max said. "Meet us at the hospital."

David's apartment was at 25th Street and Third Avenue. The hospital was on 98th and Madison. I could have run the

75 blocks, a la Billy Crystal in *When Harry Met Sally*. I could have but I didn't. I wanted to be the first grandparent there. I took a cab. When I walked in the door of the labor room on the obstetrics floor of the hospital, Lauren's parents, Stu and Helaine Shilling, who lived an hour away in New Jersey, were already there. I've never figured out how that was possible.

Max had taken command of the labor room, which was also to be the delivery room. He ordered the three of us off the set.

Helaine, Stu, and I sat in the green room, or whatever the term is for a tiny, magazine-free waiting area furnished with a few plastic chairs that appeared to be donations from a redecorated police precinct. Hours slogged by. Around 2 a.m. Helaine slipped out and found us some coffee at a nurses' station.

"This place is filthy," she said, balancing three Styrofoam cups. "They have paper plates with cat food on the floor. They have cats! That means they have mice."

Helaine worked in the neonatal department of a hospital in New Jersey. While we waited, she told stories about rodents in hospital walls that ate the wiring of the heart monitors. Surely, this was a more upscale venue.

"I heard that all the celebrities have their babies here," I said.

"They do," said Helaine. "On the eighth floor. Two thousand dollars a day extra."

Three hard-working generations from our peasant past and my grandchild was still being born in steerage.

At 6:15 a.m. I said, "You were right about the cats, Helaine. Listen."

There was a distinct, soft mewing.

"That's not a cat!" she yelled. "That's a baby!"

She shouted again to wake up Stu and we three ran down the hall toward the delivery room. Max met us at the door and paused to increase the drama.

We forced our way in. In the isolette was a glistening, pink, seven-pound boy. Cooper Jack Crisp.

"When he crowned," Max said, "it was just like a small saucer, top of his head, and then I helped Lauren, and when I looked back, there was this face! This face! Staring up, eyes wide open. A whole, entire human face! I don't know what I expected, but I'd never thought of his face. It blew my mind."

Lauren and Cooper were moved to a shared room. Behind the thin curtain separating the two families, a television was blasting with the sound of punches and tough language.

"The first day of his life and he has to be subjected to profanity and violence?" Max said. "This is not acceptable."

I mentioned that the movie on the neighbor's set was *Rocky V*, about as violent, by current standards, as *Bambi.* Max was nonplussed.

"Tell her to turn it off!"

"No!" said Lauren. "The mother is out on parole. Don't piss her off."

Max turned to us, the grandparents, and said, "You have to leave. We have to be alone. Lauren needs rest and Cooper needs less commotion."

Less commotion? What? Who is this man, if not the Commotion King?

I never believed my son would grow up.

But he did.

RENEWAL

Dan's family was old money. When we visited them,
I would arise early and dust the drywood frass—termite
poop—off their massive pieces of mahogany and walnut
Queen Anne tables and chairs.

I got a thrill out of sitting in one of the formal chairs.
Dan's many-greats-grandfather was the Englishman Robert
Southey, who, among other accomplishments as a historian
and a poet laureate of England, wrote "The Story of the
Three Bears." I have sat in a chair that held the behind of the
father of Goldilocks. And it was just right.

Old money is gracious and invisible. Dan's parents lived
in a lovely house that was indistinguishable from town after
town of lovely houses on the San Francisco Peninsula. Every
day Dan's mother wore girdles with rubber tabs to hold her
hose, and plain pumps. Her gold or pearl earrings were not
for decoration, they were for dignity: one didn't appear in
public with naked earlobes, although that is something she
never would have said, which is another admirable quality
of old money. Unless it runs for public office it keeps its
mouth shut.

And it never, ever drives a new car.

Dan's father worked with Dan's grandfather in a shared
room on the second floor of a small industrial building in

Palo Alto. Dan's father put on a suit and tie every day and left the house before 8:30 a.m. and his father followed the same routine.

The bottom floor of their company's only office was a garage. The lot on which the building was constructed was concrete and, at any given time, displayed three or four shiny used cars.

The business didn't survive on the profits from selling two or three used cars a month; it survived on the wisdom of Dan's father in managing the inheritance of Dan's mother. Dan's father was very good at the investment part of his job but his joy was buying and selling used cars. The family's joy was in the access he had to the car auctions. Everyone in the family drove a previously owned, absolutely delicious car.

Dan's sister Sylvia was my friend for life except that her life was ended by melanoma when she was 44. When we met she was driving a powder-blue '64 1/2 Mustang convertible. I was awed by Sylvia, who was effortlessly cool. She was lanky and wry and wore faded jeans and loafers without socks. She applied makeup only under duress, a respectful sense that the occasion required a spot of lipstick. Her hair blew straight off her shoulders when she drove—in my memories the convertible's top is never up—and when she put on the brakes her long straight mane fell back into place like golden brown satin drapes.

Our freshman year, when Dan dated my friend Lani, he drove a 1959 Datsun Sports S211, a small black convertible. Lani lost interest in him over the summer and didn't relent when he returned in the fall with a white '63 Ford Galaxy convertible.

Dan's mother drove a white '64 Lincoln Continental convertible with an embossed panel on the dashboard that said, "Hey, Luigi!" Dan's father attached that plaque as a surprise before he brought the car home from the auction. Luigi was a stranger who'd ridden a train with the family in Italy the summer they went on a long-planned European tour. Dan and Sylvia were teenagers. The trip, their parents knew, would be the last opportunity for everyone to share this experience together. Therefore, the trip was not cancelled even though by that summer, and much to her surprise, Dan's mother was six months' pregnant.

The Italian train was crowded. The only seats Luigi and his friend could find were on either side of Dan's mother. The conversation between the two men was continuous, contentious, and animated—"Hey, Luigi!"—arms and hands flying over her face and breasts and baby-filled abdomen.

In Italy, although the family went everywhere tourists were supposed to go and saw the Coliseum and David and the Sistine Chapel and gardens, fountains, lakes and vineyards, the lasting memory was that train ride.

Dan's father called his wife "Luigi" thereafter. When I met them four or five years after the trip, he'd shortened it to "Lu." Lu was as if a new wife, one born of shared laughter into a marriage that celebrated Italy as a midterm honeymoon, and never again recalled as the place Dan's father was during the war when she was alone on the home front with two babies, the place where he moved with the infantry, village to village, cleaning up after the Germans, the place from which he returned, modified by secrets into a man she didn't know.

In 1967, Dan and I went to his grandmother's house in Pebble Beach for Thanksgiving. After we finished eating the turkey, my father-in-law said, "Come outside, Wendy. There's something I want to show you."

Outside, a gift for me, was a blue '67 Camaro. Everyone had been in on the surprise. Their faces were anticipatory.

I constructed a wide smile. *It wasn't a convertible.*

I said, "Thank you!"

In Los Angeles Dan had been driving me to my job at *Datamation* and returning to USC for his classes. I drove in the evenings and weekends to grocery shop and do the laundry.

Now, I would travel the daytime freeways solo.

"I guess you'd better get a driver's license," Dan said.

I was 23. I'd never had a driver's license and I'd been driving everywhere since I was 16 and got an "A" in Driver's Ed.

I had wanted to get a license in July, 1959, on the day I qualified for a learner's permit. Unfortunately for me, the day that the DMV examiner came to Ferndale conflicted with the Camp Fire Girls' day camp in Fortuna, where my mother was the camp director and I was in charge of music.

"Drive me back to Ferndale," I begged and my mother said, "Don't be ridiculous. I'm not running a day camp without a song leader."

That was, sadly, the day I was ready. Three weeks later, when the examiner again made the trip down-county to set up the cones in the parking lot at the fairgrounds, I showed up for my appointment, passed the written test, and drove through the initial series of commands—"Turn left," "Make a U turn "—easily.

"Very nice," the examiner said. "Now let's see you parallel park."

I couldn't remember which way the wheels go if you steer to the right and I couldn't remember the rules about degrees of the angle at which to aim the car at the curb. In the past semester I'd been given a "C" in geometry and that was only because the teacher, a one-year hire, was a middle-aged, recently divorced man with stained ties. I suggested my mother invite him to our house for dinner. Without her tamale pie I would have been given the "D" I'd earned.

"He's an odd duck," she said when he left, and I said, "No one likes him but I can't do the Pythagorean theorem."

I failed the first driver's test I took because I was unable to parallel park and I failed it two more times that year for the same reason.

Seemed like a clear enough message, so I made the only decision available to a rejected teenager. I dumped the DMV.

Three years later, in 1962, the summer that Seattle hosted the World's Fair, Sue and I and two other 18-year-old girls rented a house on Vashon Island in Puget Sound, a location reachable only by ferry from Seattle. Before we made the first crossing we purchased a '51 Ford for $75 from a friend of Dan's.

(The prior November I'd called my mother from the dorm. "You don't have to make a decision right now," I said. "I'd like to get a summer job at the World's Fair and live in Seattle with some other girls, and…"

"That's a good idea," she said.)

Among us girls only Sue had a valid driver's license. Bardahl's had expired. Lani had a lifetime license from Hawaii that wasn't recognized on the mainland. I, of course, was in a self-imposed, eternal exile from state vehicle authority.

On four bald tires we drove the Ford around the island from one beach kegger/clam dig to another and often with the island's single cop trailing behind us.

In Pebble Beach, without even hearing the back story, the blood drained from my father-in-law's face. He's mad at me, I thought. Now, of course, I know exactly what he was thinking: *Good God, full liability exposure.*

"Yes," he said. "You will need to have a license before you drive your car."

I promptly got one. I've had a driver's license every moment of my subsequent adult life, and in 2016, it came up for a January renewal.

My friend Mary Ellen had aced her renewal in November, so she dropped the DMV book of laws and suggestions at my office and attached a yellow post-it note. "You'd better hurry up and make an appointment. They're already booked through December."

The first date I could get was January 11, my birthday and the very last day I could legally drive on my current license, a limit I now take very seriously since the full liability exposure is mine.

In recent years, renewal has been online—check this box, check that, the end. This year the DMV was asking me to submit to a new eye test and a new photograph and register a passing score on the written test. Study would be required.

In college we were on the semester system, which meant that Dan and I hauled a hundred pounds of textbooks home with us on Christmas vacations, and left them unopened for two weeks during which the tension of looming January finals distorted the concept of vacation.

One winter during those years Charles Schulz penned a series of *Peanuts* strips that told a day-by-day story of procrastination and guilt over a book report on *Moby Dick* that Charlie Brown had to turn in the day after New Year's.

With my renewal birthday looming I spent Christmas as Charlie Brown. Every day I had a reason for not opening the DMV booklet. (*You only need to scan this material; you've been driving for years, you know the answers; you have plenty of time left; how hard can this be, you just passed a course in microeconomics, for heaven's sake!*)

I tried to follow Lucy's five-cent advice. (Start with the whale.) December passed quickly into January.

The night before my 9:20 a.m. DMV appointment I opened the booklet and was happily surprised. It was clearly written, straightforward and respectful, formal and yet colloquial. I was halfway through before Lucy screamed, "This isn't an English test! What did you just read? See, you can't tell me! You're going to flunk! HAHAHA!"

I read it again and retained nothing. Fear was vandalizing my brain. Worse, I had no idea what to wear. The driver's license photograph would be something I'd have to see every day for the next ten years. I didn't want it to be a downer, like that 1999 Costco card where I'm smiling this big grin but something went haywire in the machine and deleted all my teeth.

Monday didn't begin well. When I stopped in town for a coffee-to-go I realized I'd left my wallet with my driver's license at home. Focusing on the rules for safe driving, I made the roundtrip to Centerville, after which I had to stop at the gas station because now the tank was lower than I'd planned.

At the gas station, Jerry, the owner, said, "You don't want to hear what happened to me at the DMV," and then he told me anyway, about three trips to Eureka, a doctor's note, and rude DMV employees.

I was leaving town much later than I had intended and I suddenly became aware I had no idea how to get to the DMV. Once, years before I knew what a meme was, I had a meme for the DMV's address. What was it? *French burgundy*. The color I dyed my hair in the summer I was 15. 15th and Summer! Good work! How do I get there?

A route I guessed might work was blocked by construction. I pulled over on a Eureka street so dicey you could shoot zombie movies there without casting and consulted Google maps.

Saved. I arrived on time and only three people were ahead of me.

I cruised through the forms and the eye test and was sent to Window 15, where a calm and kind woman took my photo. (Every employee at the DMV was welcoming—Jerry may live in a parallel universe.)

Only the test remained. I stepped up to a cubicle with a computer monitor and placed my thumb on an optical fingerprint reader. Yes! My thumb passed; surely my brain would follow.

It didn't. Of the first five questions, I missed the maximum allowable—three—and the computer stopped. *Test over.*

I returned to Window 15. Now there were eleven people ahead of me. I was hungry, I'd left my phone in the coffee compartment in my car, and I was finding it hard to make friends.

When my turn came I had to say, loudly, "I didn't pass the test."

"Do you want to take it again now?" another nice employee asked.

"I have to," I said. "My license expires today and I live in Ferndale, at the beach, it's too far, and my husband will have to come and get me and drive me around until I can pass and…"

Get a grip! If your mascara runs into your eyes you won't be able to see the test, let alone pass it!

"Yes."

I reminded myself not to over-think the questions. (The correct answers to most of the questions posed by the California Department of Motor Vehicles are: N*ever do this or you will be fined all your money, you will go to jail, and you will lose your license forever.* The other answers are .08 percent, 18 inches, and "only for emergencies.")

I passed because, in the end, the DMV exam is not a book report on *Moby Dick.* For five more years I can drive some version of a leased gray Honda Accord, a car that blends so well with others in the parking lots I have to push the key button that activates the horn so I can find it, flashing and honking, like a lost animal crying for its mother. Sometimes I attempt to break into other people's cars. (When did I pick up the dry cleaning? Who borrowed my car and ate at Burger King?) My car is practical, fuel-efficient, easy to parallel park.

But it's not a convertible.

SNOW DAYS

As I awake I hear a car move pass the house, its tires swishing, spitting—the sounds of a dentist's office.

Snow.

"It's not going to last long," Lauren says. "It's supposed to start raining. The mountain road is going to be pure ice."

On this day, up the mountain road in Highland Falls, the hometown of West Point, Max and Lauren are opening a fast casual restaurant they have named American Burrito.

Cooper and Carson, nine and seven, sit on the sofa and watch a television show amped with canned laughter. The edited chortling was recorded decades earlier. They are listening to dead people laughing.

On the screen a teenage girl says something about popcorn balls that rings familiar.

"Didn't we watch this show last night?" I ask.

"That's what they do," Lauren says. "They watch the same thing over and over. *Madagascar 3*? Four times in one weekend. This is 'Good Luck, Charlie.' It's a series. They'll watch it all day."

It was 7:30 a.m. The boys were in their pajamas. Max had left for West Point at 4:30 a.m. There was an absence of urgency in the house. In a gothic novel it would be preternaturally calm.

"School?" I ask.

"There's a two-hour delay because of the snow. So why go at all when you're here? They get a chance to stay home with Nana."

Four eyes don't stray from "Good Luck, Charlie," but four ears flicker like wild deer.

Lauren gives me instructions and shows me the food, explaining what is immediately edible and what is reserved for school lunches. She reminds me how to use the controls for the electronics and points out the spot in the snow where the dogs are allowed to pee.

The Wheaton terriers, Gatsby and Ruby, are curled together under the coffee table in a sleepy heap.

Lauren leaves the house. As soon as her Jeep rolls out of the driveway Ruby ambles into the bathroom and pees on the floor.

The boys, too, heard the secret signal. Within seconds the floor is strewn with boxes of board games and Hedbanz has begun.

"I am a unicorn!" Carson screams.

"Did you think he was a unicorn, Nana? That was a stupid unicorn."

I am sitting on the floor, endangered by the punching ball of boys.

In an effort to stand up, my left foot upends a bowl of M&M peanuts. Gatsby is aroused.

"Chocolate is bad for dogs," I say. Canned laughter follows my comment.

We adjourn to the nearby playroom, where a second screen looms over two camp chairs and two bean-bag chairs. The walls are covered with posters of extraordinarily buff men.

"Sit here, Nana," Carson says. I lower myself slowly into a black bean-bag chair.

Cooper is concentrating on the controls for a video game. He hands me a black plastic remote.

"What's your favorite video game, Nana?" Carson asks.

I haven't played a video game since Ms. PacMan. I liked that one. I was addicted to it for an entire summer vacation that I spent at Cuba Lake, ninety miles south of Buffalo. Every day I rowed across the lake and played Ms. PacMan on the machine at the gas station. Ms. PacMan had to outrun puffy pastel ghosts who were trying to kill her. When the vacation was over I returned to Manhattan and resigned as the editor of *Savvy*.

"This game is about professional wrestling," Cooper said. "Who do you like?"

Oh, dig sweet synapses, find a name. Gorgeous George? Even Max is too young for that one. Try again. The Hulk.

"The Hulk?"

"Good one, Nana!" Cooper said, and Carson said, "I hate The Hulk."

I had no idea how to operate the toggle switches and buttons on the remote. Cooper gave me a quick lesson, informed Carson that his turn came after mine.

"I'm John Cena," he says. "You can be The Hulk."

The virtual image of John Cena was making some kind of sign.

"What's he doing with his fingers?"

"This is just like real life. That's what he does in real life."

"He makes the peace sign?"

X-Box John Cena raises both arms, spreads his hands, and in each hand makes a circle with his thumb and his index finger.

This gesture triggers whoops from the boys, laughter that in no way resembles the scratchy cacklings of the dead that still underscore every line I can clearly hear in the Disney program no one is watching.

"His fingers spell a bad word," Cooper says.

"A-s-s," says Carson. "And the circle—"

"I get it," I say. "How rude."

John Cena throws The Hulk to the mat and The Hulk, poorly toggled by me, is helpless. Game over. Next we're choosing college football teams, selecting uniform colors. I've barely figured out a flying headlock and now I'm a quarterback for Boise State.

"Select a play!" Cooper yells. "Hurry up!"

The screen offers me a list of plays. The only one I recognize is a Hail Mary. I select it. I lose.

"You can't do that without a receiver," Cooper says, with condescension. How sad it must be to live life as Nana, someone who has the Heisman in more or less the same brain cell as Heineken, Heimlich and Himmler.

"I'm putting on a show tonight," Carson announces. "Here's your ticket. It's not a real ticket, it's a pass. You're getting in free."

The show will be in the living room. In the detritus of Hedbanz a rehearsal takes place. On an iPad Cooper composes the music, a heavy rock score with piano, drums, and guitar.

Carson changes from Kung-Fu Panda pajamas into the garments of a Mongol invader. He leaps onto an ottoman and sings an original song that has something to do with "stopping on the road in flames."

The rehearsal continues. I explain apologetically that I have a column due to an editor in California in a couple of hours. I set my laptop on the coffee table. Ruby sprawls over my right arm. Occasionally she types something. Gatsby lies on my left foot and snarls. The M&Ms aren't settling well, if one can believe the olfactory evidence.

Lauren returns from the grand opening in West Point in midafternoon.

"Get ready," she says. "The Cub Scouts are going to White Plains to see the Harlem Globetrotters."

"On these roads?" I ask.

"They've got salt out. Dress warm. It's going to be one degree before midnight."

"One? One Farenheit?"

"Yeah, but they say it will feel like minus 17. Take a scarf."

In the parking lot of the Westchester Civic Center, I exit the car and walk on the salted ice. It's not flat, it's more like a flash-frozen ocean. As I carefully move toward the stadium, I'm muttering the survival chant of elders. *Don't fall, don't break your hip, your children won't take care of you.*

Inside the gym I recognized the venue. I was here in 1986, when Max was 11.

He was a sixth grader on the Fox Lane Middle School basketball team and his coach, who had expansive, egocentric aspirations, scheduled a game with a team from Yonkers. Geographically and athletically, the match was from outer space. Over parental protest, the game lasted the full four quarters. The final score was 128-3, Yonkers. The MVP for Fox Lane was Ryan, who made the three free-throws.

Awaiting the Globetrotters, the echoing thumps of dribbling in a mist of sweat evoked other basketball memories.

In the fall of 1966, *Datamation's* Los Angeles offices were on West Olympic Boulevard across the street from a three-story motel that may have been called the Olympian. Professional athletes stayed there because it was convenient to both the Forum, where the Lakers played basketball, and the Coliseum, where the Rams played football.

The tavern at the Olympian was a slice of heaven for the men in our office, a real-time sports bar on the biggest television set available in 1966. As the games were mostly on film and not live, it was not uncommon to be sitting near an actual player.

("Over there!" I whispered to Heide, the secretary, one day when we were sharing a club sandwich in the bar. "All those midgets coming in!"

"Those people aren't midgets," Heide said. "The guy they're with is Wilt Chamberlain.")

Datamation had four season-ticket floor seats to the Lakers games for the purpose of entertaining advertisers. On the few nights when no advertisers were in town, one of the salesmen would stroll out to the reception area and toss a couple tickets on my desk.

This was a significant bonus; a pair of tickets cost seventy-five percent of my monthly take-home pay.

Dan and I became serious Laker fans. I loved Jerry West and, when the Cincinnati Royals were in town, Oscar Robertson.

And there was the matter of Doris Day. She and her boyfriend, Dodger shortstop Maury Wills, sat in the floor seats next to the team, directly across the court from our seats. The line of vision was perfect and I was close enough to see her turquoise eye shadow. (In her autobiography, I am obliged to note, Doris denies she was Maury Wills' girlfriend. In any case, they were, at the very least, "long-time hoop-side companions.")

One afternoon, Bob Forest suggested we all go over to the Olympian and have a drink. Those were "Mad Men" days—everybody drank hard liquor during work hours.

When I joined *Datamation* I had just graduated from college where I had consumed a lot of beer, sometimes mixed with bourbon into a boilermaker, which made me throw up. Throwing up was awkward—it wrecked my makeup—but it was not a deterrent. In those pre-pill years panty girdles were the deterrent.

College boozing was not career cocktails.

Now living in a garden apartment that Dan and I had rented after escaping the concrete towers of the USC married students' housing, I asked my landlady—who was 70, almost too old to give me confidence in her advice—what I should order to maintain both my newly minted adult facade and my dignity. She suggested that on business occasions I order sherry. I drank Dry Sack for years before I learned about fortified wine and realized that contrary to sherry being a conservative choice, I had tripled the chances of disgracing myself.

The magazine staff trooped across Olympic Boulevard and sat down at a long table to talk, drink, and watch a professional basketball re-run on the big TV.

"What would Martians think of us," Bob joked, "if they were to land and find a culture that is serious about men who run up and down in a small room trying to put a ball through a net?"

"Yeah," I said. "In their underwear."

Everyone roared with laughter. Bob smashed his Scotch mist on the table, stood up, and pointed at me.

"Don't you ever step on my lines again," he said, and walked out.

I could have used a Dry Sack at the Cub Scout outing to the Globetrotters. I was seated on a low, broken stadium chair that pitched slightly forward, plus it had been temporarily erected behind a portable backstop, an obstacle that created a split view of the action, like seeing the game through a video stereopticon.

The pregame program lasted for 90 minutes. Endlessly, the announcer screamed into the microphone, a barrage of unintelligible jokes that were physically acted out on center court by earth-globe-headed mascots. The announcer's jokes were punctuated with the rhetorical "Are you ready to rumble?"

I finally yelled, "I was ready an hour ago," a reaction that so enchanted the Cub Scout granddad on my right that he gave me a pretzel.

Hours later, at home and warm, I decided I'd had a wonderful time. I remembered that the Harlem Clowns, a second-tier version of the Globetrotters, had come to Ferndale in the 1950s. Everyone in the valley drove into town to the high school gym to watch them.

Professional basketball wasn't on television yet, not that we would have known. Most families in the valley didn't own a TV set.

We were fascinated by the slam dunks, fancy dribbling, and sleight-of-hand passing, astonished to watch very tall black men, gentle, agile, exotic giants, dancing to "Sweet Georgia Brown." I sat next to my aunt, transfixed, a mere fluff of a dandelion seed in the midst of magic.

When I was perched in the wobbly stadium seat I'd wondered if Cooper and Carson and the other boys in Cub Scout Pack 46 would be so impressed. What can awe the children of today? They play virtual sports videos. They go to dozens of pro football, baseball, and basketball games. They watch never-ending ESPN.

When the Globetrotters exhibition was over, a player with the name "Big Shot" on the back of his shirt gave his sweaty headband to Carson. Turbo, another player, shook hands with Cooper and posed for a selfie with the boys, Lauren, and me. The boys were reverent. Cooper gave me a warning look, as if I were unaware of the holiness of the moment.

Lauren posted the selfie on Facebook. Her friends "liked" it. I didn't.

I was wearing four bulky sweaters under my jacket and my eyes were shut. And fluorescent lighting?

Maury Wills wouldn't have given me a second glance.

THE OTHER GRANDMOTHER

Helaine, my grandsons' other grandmother, died on Friday, June 15, 2012.

Eleven years earlier, a few months before the house she and Stuart were building for their retirement was completed and five months before Max and Lauren's wedding, she was diagnosed with stage four ovarian cancer.

She lived to move into her house, to attend the wedding, to be there for the births of a third granddaughter and two grandsons, and to watch all five grandchildren enter school. Helaine lived to participate in her oldest granddaughter's bat mitzvah in 2011, even though doing so required having three blood transfusions in three days so she could stand, fragile and beautiful, and listen to Ashley perform the long service in Hebrew so perfect the old men were dumbstruck.

Helaine was with Robyn and Lauren and their families for every holiday and celebration, and for most vacations.

The week of her death, Sue and I had driven to Seattle to celebrate the fiftieth anniversary of the summer we'd spent on Vashon Island. Lauren called to say her mother had only days to live.

Lauren and Robyn had been at her bedside 24 hours a day for a week. They slept together in the king-sized bed in their parents' room, sisters, women, mothers, wives, little girls, crying and talking and laughing and crying again, as their mother lay on a gurney by Robyn's side.

I left the car with my Seattle friends, Sue flew home to Los Angeles, and I went to Newark, New Jersey, my plane greeted by John, who was already there to attend a grandson's graduation.

"She's still alive," I said, "and I wanted to see her but Max says no, she's not conscious and the girls have enough to cope with without me being there."

Helaine died the next day.

"Why didn't you call sooner?" I asked Lauren and she said, "We didn't want you here sooner. It was like she was waiting for you to get here before she could go. I knew if somehow she knew you were here, she'd die. And she did."

I had never been to a graveside service. John and I drove from the funeral home to the cemetery, and as we neared the site, I was annoyed to see a dump truck parked to one side of the grave by a huge, apparently abandoned pile of soil. Three shovels were stuck in the dirt.

They could have tidied up, I mumbled.

The rabbi stood by the grave surrounded by 50 or 60 mourners. Recognizing that some of us were not Jewish, he explained the tradition.

"We cover the coffin," he said, "filling the grave completely ourselves. We think of it as tucking in someone we love, saying goodbye. It is a final act of love that we do not want to put in the hands of strangers."

Everyone was welcome, he added, to either put in a shovel or two of dirt or, in a more intimate gesture, a handful.

Helaine's husband Stu stepped forward first, then Lauren, Robyn, then Max and Scott. A line formed.

I could see the tops of the heads of Ashley, Taylor, and Morgan, Robyn and Scott's daughters, as they moved forward. Other close relatives followed. I waited for the appropriate opportunity to slip in, and at last, seeing what appeared to be a space between two men, I stepped up.

The space wasn't empty. Standing solemnly in his black suit, eyes fixed on the open pit in front of him, was six-year-old Carson, my grandson. Helaine's grandson.

His turn came. With both hands he reached and clasped the dirt, crumbling the soil in his fingers gently before releasing it to drift to the coffin below.

MAIN STREET

On a clear, end-of-summer Tuesday, I left the office at 3:00 with plans to stop at the Valley Grocery and the liquor store on my way home.

We were out of mozzarella, my single local option for soft cheese. I was planning to make chiles rellenos from our neighbor's fresh poblanos. I needed anisette as well to make cookbook author Patricia Wells's bistro dish that begins with a 24-hour marinade of chicken legs and thighs in fresh tomatoes, fennel, garlic, and Pernod. Patricia Wells may casually pour Pernod over Costco chicken, but I'd be forced to drink it to justify the expense.

"I'll be home at 3:30," I said to John on the last second of my cell phone's battery.

Then I dropped off the face of the earth

During the office day I'd forgotten about the repaving of Main Street or, as the California Department of Transportation (and no one else) calls it, State Route 211. We call it the road to Fernbridge, the most well-traveled road in and out of town. After it passes the city limits of Ferndale, State Route 211 becomes Main Street.

On this sunny day, a road crew was covering Main Street in steaming black tar. For a few blocks I was able to bypass the mess by weaving through the alleys that connect short residential side streets with random historical names: Tennyson, Madison, Lincoln.

There are thousands of reasons not to raise children in the suburbs and the absence of alleys may be reason number one. Even though I was behind the wheel of an automobile, I felt the rush of my elementary school years, that long, golden time between seven and 12, when we moved through the world in packs, peering into back yards, eavesdropping on adult conversations, picking apples and plums from the trees that hung over the weathered fences, exploring empty sheds, avoiding or seeking other wildings. We wandered from the alleys to the creek, found birds' nests and brush-covered bridges, and became shape-shifting characters in the endless adventure that fueled our days.

Startling me out of my reverie, I hear, "Miss! Miss!"

A Caltrans traffic controller on duty at the high school was in no mood for daydreamers. Good for her. I was in no mood to be T-boned by a logging truck.

Traffic on the unpaved section of Main Street was sparse. As I approached downtown, I saw no one. It looked like the scene from *On the Beach*, where Gregory Peck, as the captain of an Australian submarine, surfaces at San Diego to see if anyone has survived a nuclear holocaust. San Diego is pristine and unblemished and not a living thing is visible.

I parked in the city lot and walked around the corner to score the mozzarella.

On the sidewalk two doors down from the Valley Grocery was Ferndale Clothing Company's 50-80%-off sales rack. I was distracted, and before I could escape owner Karen had me in her web, and I was in the dressing room struggling with two models' coats and a teal cardigan.

I carried my loot to the counter where an unfamiliar woman was dangling a toy on a string before the store's cat.

Behind her back I frowned and contorted my face into expressions of "Who's that?" and "Cat toys, are you kidding me?"

"Wendy, meet Fran," Karen said. Karen has been the president of the Chamber of Commerce for more than 25 years. She is happiest when everyone in town is getting along, especially if they're doing it while shopping.

"Fran is visiting from Prescott, Arizona," Karen continued. "She's hanging out here for while with us, waiting for her husband. He's gone to Fortuna."

I wondered why he'd gone to Fortuna. Jerry's gas station was open. Tom could fill a prescription. What could a tourist need across the river? And on a day when the only way to get out of town was covered with steaming tar?

I smiled at Fran, the kind of smile that said, "Please don't tell me about your cat back home."

"There's not a single car parked on either side of the street for as far as you can see," I said to Karen. "It's spooky, and my cell phone is dead. Will you take a picture?"

Karen's no-car photo of Main Street will be worth a million dollars in the 22nd century. Researchers, in the way that history telescopes to absurdity, will debate what could have happened. Why is there a narrow tarmac on the east side? Could an airborne missile landing have been anticipated? Was it a race track for a fossil-fuel vehicle?

Karen asked me a business question, I gave a long answer and while Karen's cat continued to hypnotize the toy-dangler, we rambled into general topics of life and love. A cowboy walked in. He was depressed because he'd just written a novel using an "I found these letters" device and he was in hot water because people thought it was true, and when he said it was fiction everyone said he'd written a bunch of lies.

Outside the sun was lower so I reached into the bag and retrieved the teal cardigan. What was it I had needed at the grocery story?

Mozzarella. And something else.

First, here was Lino, crossing Main Street, heading my way.

"Hey," I said. "I've been meaning to call you. I talked to Art last week and he said how his parents used to go visit the Gabriellis all the time. Several people have said how they'd like to see the old place so John and I have decided to invite everyone who grew up visiting the Gabriellis, all you old, just kidding, Italians, to come back and visit the ranch.

Jim Pegolotti's coming out for Antone's 90th birthday. Maybe that's a good time. We'll make lunch."

"Sounds good," said Lino, and he told me a long story about his mother and how she and a baby boy were turned away at Ellis Island because the infant had spinal meningitis, and by the time they had landed back in Italy the boy was dead, and she had to wait a year before she could return to America, and she'd already crossed the Atlantic twice before because her father had taken the family from Italy to Brazil and then changed his mind.

"And that is why," Lino said, "the farthest she'd ever go from home after that was the six-mile trip from the farm in Grizzly Bluff to the Gabrielli dairy at Centerville."

I was listening and I was doing an internal chant: *mozzarella, mozzarella, mozzarella and something else.*

Inside the Valley Grocery, I picked up the cheese, and a lemon, and some Italian flat-leafed parsley. Something else…a bag of licorice whips triggered the brain cell. Anisette.

"I need a cheap bottle," I told Paul at the liquor store. "It's for the chicken."

"Lucky chicken," Paul said.

I was able to remember where I'd parked the car because I was wearing the teal sweater from the sales rack.

Two hours after I'd left my office I arrived home.

"I thought you were on your way a while ago," John said.

"I was," I said. "But I had to pick up some cheese."

CELEBRITIES

The phone rang in the early moments of a balmy, seductive twilight. John and I were sitting on the deck with glasses of Marsala.

It was Max, calling from New York. Max calls me three or four times a year.

He was croaking hoarsely at the other end of the line.

"Can you hear me? Everyone here is asleep. I'm trying to be quiet. Okay, you do know what my favorite TV show is, right?"

No, I don't. We haven't talked for so long my guess is "The Brady Bunch." I don't say that. I say, "Remind me."

"My whole life, best show on television, 'NFL Classic Games.' I've seen them all, dozens of times. So I come home tonight, grab a beer, sit down to watch, and it's the 2008 playoff game from Green Bay. Giants and Packers."

His voice was rising.

Max and Lauren and the boys live in a cottage. I'm wondering how the rest of the family can be sleeping through both a football game and Max "whispering."

"Do you remember that game?"

Sure. Like it was yesterday. Who could forget the Packers. Are they still called the Packers? Does anyone actually pack anything there anymore? What was it they packed in the beginning? Sturgeon? Or is that just the Bay? No, probably meat trucked up from the Chicago stockyards.

"Pay attention. That's the game Scott and I went to."

Now I remember. It was too expensive for the family to fly out for Christmas, but by some Yuletide miracle there was enough money for Max and Scott to fly from New York to Green Bay, Wisconsin, to see the NFL playoff game that would determine who would play in Superbowl XLII.

"It was 25 below zero out there!" Max was saying. "I told you, Scott's hands nearly fell off with frostbite. I got a cup of hot coffee and by the second sip it went down frozen and destroyed my esophagus. Best weekend of our lives. The Giants won, 23-20, in overtime. Brett Favre's last game with the Packers. Epic, friggin' epic."

"Why do you say 'Farve' when the 'v' comes before the 'r'? Why isn't it 'fav-ree'?"

"Just listen. I'm sitting here in my tighty whities, watching 'NFL Classic Games,' as usual, and that playoff game is featured. Okay, I'm already totally psyched, waiting for the end, and suddenly I'm on TV! ON TV. I'm in the friggin' broadcast. There I am, high-fiving Umenyiora..."

"What?"

"Umenyiora. Osi Umenyiora. Defensive end? Try a little here, okay? I'm high-fiving him, it's the glamour shot, end of the game. There I am, I mean there I am! Historic NFL moment, one of the greatest games ever played and I'm on the screen with Osi Umenyiora! My wife isn't speaking to me."

She was speaking to someone. I could hear her in the background. She grabbed the phone.

"Wendy, I'm telling you, I thought we'd won the lottery. The boys and I are sleeping. I'm in a deep sleep, you know how hard it is to get any sleep with kids? And suddenly this mad man in his underwear is jumping around the house screaming! He's red-faced, yelling, laughing, sweating. We're millionaires, I think. Multi-millionaires. Let me put it in perspective for you. If I look very hard I can see someone in a brown jacket—is it brown? Not sure—at the end of a row of seats, hanging over the edge. Maybe it's Max, maybe not, and it's not on ESPN, it's on ESTN, something like that. A cable show so far off the grid they don't even spell the name of the network right…"

The phone is repossessed.

"She's embellishing. It's on ESPN 2. And you can see me, up front and clearly, and for a long time. I re-watched it on TiVO and timed it. It's one-Mississippi, two-Mississippi, three-Mississippi, easily. There I am, center of the screen in one of the great NFL games of all time on a broadcast that will be watched forever. I mean, history, this is a friggin' documentary. America, folks, America."

That was last night. Today I'm more knowledgeable. I Googled Osi Umenyiora. He was born in London to Nigerian parents. They moved to Auburn, Alabama, where he started playing football. He's from the Igbo tribe and in Igbo his name means "from today, things will be good."

I'm downloading the January 20, 2008 NFL playoff game in which Osi Umenyiora is seen for three full seconds high-fiving Maximilian Waldner Crisp, whose name means "loving people who like to laugh."

When Osi sees that clip he's going to jump right out of his underwear.

THE 70-POUND PUPPY

I'm counting the days—21—until Sara arrives from San Diego to collect Jake, her Akbash puppy we've been fostering for five months.

Someone—you know who you are—decided not to adopt Francis Sweet's puppies. Francis saw John at the men's prayer breakfast and offered us one "for free."

John said yes, because Sara, whose house burned to the ground in a wildfire in 2007, who lived in other people's houses and in a small trailer for six years until the new house was finished, Sara, whose husband died suddenly five months after they moved into the new house, who bought Moose, an adult Akbash, to keep her company until he died young of cancer—Sara is ready for another dog. Another Akbash.

Francis's little boy fit the bill perfectly, except for the timing. Sara had trips planned to Scotland (her home country), Mexico (to see the monarch butterflies), and to Burma. She couldn't take delivery of Jake until the middle of June.

"No problem," said John.

The Akbash is a livestock protector dog that bonds with sheep and keeps them safe from coyotes and mountain lions and crows. When we had sheep we had two Akbashes.

Buddy the brave died of bone cancer when he was four; Moose, a slacker, we sold to Sara. Moose never liked sheep. They'd wander off and he'd glance up from the porch and yawn. He never moved, he never barked.

There are coyotes in the rolling hills of Escondido. Sara doesn't care. She doesn't have sheep. In his new, royal role, Moose had been able to walk to the side of the wrap-around, poured concrete deck, raise his nose slightly, and woof before wandering back into the house to listen to Swedish jazz. Before he died of lymphoma, Moose was featured above the fold in a four-color photograph in the "Mansions" section of the *Wall Street Journal*. All of this is true.

The Akbash breed, native to Turkey, is thought to originate from a single line coming out of central Asia in the time of the Mongols. Europe boasts many breeds that are likely family members: Anatolian shepherd, Great Pyrenees, Komondor, Kuvasz, Cuvac, Ovtcharka. The breed, minus the occasional slacker, is vigilant, intelligent and calm.

The Akbash will neutralize threats to the flock with speed, grace, and overwhelming power. A ditz from the City showed up a few years ago with a Rottweiler. The Rott jumped out of her Subaru, raced to the back yard and immediately killed six chickens, and headed to the pastures, a lamb in his crosshairs. Buddy, a full field away, raced like a greyhound, soundless and swift, and reached the Rott before it reached the lamb. No snarling, no growling, no unseemly violence. Buddy flattened the intruder with one paw.

The breed is immense. It's the Dodge Power Wagon of dogs. Jake is five-and-a-half months old and he weighs 70 pounds. He's very happy when I come home from work. He runs into the driveway at the speed of light and knocks me over. And if that isn't a constant barrel of fun, he's cutting teeth, and his chew-toy of choice is our sprinkler system, a teething ring of black tubing.

Jake has been ingenious in creating his own living space. In the front yard, in what I used to call the garden, he's made a homeless encampment.

From the clothesline in the backyard, he's dragged blankets from the guest room and spread them on the ground. Around the edges of the blankets he has placed attractive femurs, mandibles, and skulls. Straw mats from the burn pile were shredded into thousands of strands and artfully scattered on the adjacent lawn, where he has already begun landscaping by digging several holes to China. Two empty Tupperware containers, the handle of a shovel, a pair of green rubber gloves, a partially eaten bag of whole wheat macaroni, and more black tubing complete the eclectic décor.

"What's he eating?" John asked.

I looked out the window.

"I don't know," I said. "I can't think of anything edible that's navy blue."

The telephone rang.

"Wendy, Sara. I don't want to alarm you but you know I was able to recover from the broken hip in time to go to Burma with Ralph. Now, I'm supposed to be in Scotland and I'm not, because while I was at rehab for the hip I slipped— and to break my fall and protect that precious hip I put out my arm and landed on it. On a scale of one to ten I have a 'ten' wrist fracture, and—"

"Can you drive? Do you want me to fly down and drive you up here to get Jake? Do you want me to drive you back to San Diego and I'll fly home?"

"I think I'll be able to drive by the middle of June and if not—"

"If not, we're here for you, Sara. We'll move heaven and earth to make sure you don't have to spend another minute without this precious, sweet, little love. Jakey, your mommy is on the phone. Oh, Sara, I wish you could see his face—wait, I've got my cell, I'll take a photo—smile for mommy, Jakey…"

I left for work and stumbled on the edge of the front porch. Half a board had been eaten since last night.

Twenty-one more days.

ATONEMENT

I'm sitting with two other people around the table in Lauren's dining room in Rockland County, New York, across the Tappan Zee Bridge from Manhattan, as far from Manhattan as Ferndale, when all is said and done, because I'm not here to sit in intimate neighborhood bars and discuss theater. I'm here to visit Lauren and Max and their boys.

It's important to Cooper and Carson to have memories of shared moments with Nana, especially since the death of Helaine, their only other grandmother. (Thanks to my hard work over the years, the boys have grandfathers in abundance.)

Right now the three of us are sharing one of Dante's nine circles of hell.

Cooper is looking at football statistics on his iPhone instead of memorizing the differences among anthropology, archaeology and paleontology. Carson is not writing a reading response to a Nate the Great mystery. He's drawing a picture of the new dog, an Airedale named Libby. I am writing my weekly column for the *Ferndale Enterprise*. I had emailed the editor, Caroline, and asked her if I was correct in my assumption that this was a week I had arranged for a bye, and she buzzed back *Nooooo!*

So here we sit, a fourth-grader, a sixth-grader, and me, who would be in grade 67 if I hadn't quit school after grade

16, the three of us inside on a clear-blue-sky day with the sun already angled and cool in autumnal hours.

Through the window I can see the basketball hoop.

"Maybe we can go outside and shoot baskets," I say in what I consider *sotto voce*.

"Not until their homework is done! Carson, what are the challenge words?"

The ears of motherhood.

I make an I'm-sorry grimace. Cooper exaggerates the same face and does things with his fingers and nose at Carson.

"Mom!"

"Cooper, stop tormenting him!"

The eyes of motherhood.

Today is Yom Kippur, the holiest day in the Jewish calendar, a day of fasting and atonement and going to temple. Children are exempted from fasting and so are old people, and, of course, people of another faith.

Nevertheless, it doesn't seem right to eat just because I qualify as an aging outsider. I pondered this most of the morning and finally decided, after eating a four-cracker snack-pack of peanut-butter-and-cheese, to fast the remaining seven hours until sundown.

It's not as if I don't need a day of atonement and repentance. I believe the humility and acceptance of moral responsibility is appreciated regardless of whether it's uttered in a temple or a confessional or muttered by a Methodist.

I love the Jewish holidays. They're rooted in Biblical tradition, they're raucous, and they're delicious.

The family that gathers at Scott and Robyn's house includes some mix of Max and Lauren and the boys, Scott and Robyn and their daughters, grandfather Stu, and often either Scott's mother Ellen, or Scott's father Jerry and his second wife Rachelle. And, occasionally, me.

At the first Passover I attended, several years before Helaine died, Scott's bifurcated family was elsewhere, so Max and I were asked to give two of the readings.

We were eager to participate. Protestants, regardless of the centuries that have passed, enjoy the rebellious feeling of reading the Bible aloud, as if the Reformation were an event from 1968. Also, the books of the Pentateuch are especially comforting: the stories are familiar and the world is more and more the same as it is today. Max read his passage beautifully. I was focused solely on mother-pride and not on the Word of God. When it came my turn I, too, was doing very well indeed until I heard a squeak from Robyn. I looked up. Stu and Helaine and their daughters were trying not to laugh.

Scott gave a stern call-to-order and I proceeded to the end of the reading with considerably reduced confidence.

When the rituals ended, there was an avalanche of laughter.

"So, it's pronounced 'om-NIP-o-tent'," Helaine said. "We've said 'omny-poTENT' our whole lives."

Lauren's family regards me as a minor celebrity. They are not off-put because the newspaper for which I write has a circulation less than that of the *New York Times*. What does concern them is that I do not mention them in every column.

Stuart, who had only been in one story, ambushed me at Rosh Hashanah several years ago.

"I was a Brownie," he said. "In our family, there was just my twin sister Susan and myself, and my mother was the Brownie leader. She made me be a Brownie instead of a Cub Scout."

"Hmmm," I said. I reached for the bowl of chopped liver.

"So does that make the column?"

"I'll think about it, Stu," I said. "But I can't promise anything. You're not from Ferndale and I was a Camp Fire Girl."

"You've already been in the column, Stu," said Scott. "I've never been in the column and she's been at our house for all the holidays."

"Not all the holidays," I said. "I wasn't here for Chanukah." I was thinking about how I should have been there for Chanukah, considering how much I love potato pancakes.

"And I don't pressure you, do I?" asked Scott. I shook my head. It's hard to answer with a mouthful of noodle kugel.

"Want to hear a joke?"

"She doesn't put jokes in the column, Scott," said Lauren. "She puts in stories. Like the one about when Cooper was born."

"That was hilarious," said Helaine. Helaine was the star of the Cooper-is-born story.

"You always write about Helaine."

"Ma is funnier than you are, Dad."

"I can be funny. Watch this."

"Stu, that's gross."

Faith is a player in New York. The culture "back east" still reflects and honors its Old World roots. The stranger is asked, "What are you?" and she is expected to respond with both an ethnic and a faith response, "Russian Jew," or "Irish Catholic."

In the late 19th Century, Cathay, North Dakota, had a hardware store owned by my grandfather, Maximilian Folendorf, and a grain elevator, a railroad station and, separated by one short block, a Methodist church and a Baptist church.

Max Folendorf was a Methodist and his wife Minna was a Baptist. In 1892 they were married in the Baptist church. They didn't attend church together again for 43 years. In my adoptive family, the Detlefsens, grandfather Jimmy was an immigrant from Schleswig-Holstein, a German-speaking Dane who went to St. Mark's, the German Lutheran church a block from our house. My grandmother Katrina was a devoted member of Our Savior's, the Danish Lutheran church. The Danish service was over long before the German one, so every Sunday Katrina drove the Essex to our house and waited for Jimmy to walk up the street. When I returned home from Sunday school at the Congregational church, she'd be sitting quietly at the kitchen table with her folded hands resting below her ample bosom.

As for my Robertson relatives, my paternal bloodline, well, therein hangs an even stranger tale.

My grandfather, John D. Robertson, Sr., was from a family of Scottish Presbyterians who wandered undocumented over the Canadian border and into Ohio where most of them did quite well for themselves, especially my great-uncle David, "Uncle Dyke," to whom, legend has it, President Franklin D. Roosevelt had promised the cabinet post of Secretary of Labor, only to renege in the end and give the job to Frances Perkins, a woman. I was told the story many times by my grandmother Ethel, an unapologetic feminist who delighted in schadenfreude, especially when her in-laws were involved.

"Your great-grandmother, Permelia Charles, was arrested in New York City while marching with the suffragettes," Ethel told me. She gave details of violence and jails and drew a vivid portrait of the middle-aged Civil War widow as a fierce, self-sacrificing advocate for womankind. I loved this story and I am not sorry that I believed it for over 60 years, up until the day I learned on Ancestry.com that Permelia Charles had been a cook in a mental hospital in southwest Pennsylvania.

Ethel claimed to be Pennsylvania Dutch, which as a child, I understood to be German with folk art.

I accepted the anecdotal evidence and without DNA testing, determined that the Robertson genetic cocktail, when mixed with my mother's (one-sixteenth French and fifteen-sixteenths German), leaves me one-thirty-second French, one-quarter Scot, and twenty-three thirty-seconds German.

One of the joys of the cultural revolution of the late '60s was the freedom for indistinguishable white people to randomly adopt everyone else's food, music, fashion and idioms.

This masquerade worked well for me until 1979, when I moved from Los Angeles to New York.

"Whaddaya? Irish?"

"No. German, mostly. Some Scot."

"Nah. You're Irish."

"I am not Irish."

I was a *Datamation* editor in a division of Dun & Bradstreet that was overwhelmingly Irish Catholic. It would have behooved me to embrace the labeling. I didn't. On St. Patrick's Day I wore orange and stayed behind in the office while everyone else tromped down Fifth Avenue in the parade.

Ethel Robertson was known by her children and grandchildren to be a cold, judgmental woman with a sharp tongue, a vicious letter-writer who held deep prejudices, most of which were targeted toward anyone who was, as she said, her lips tensing to a wrinkled line, *Roman* Catholic.

She outlived her husband by seven years and, in 1970, died a lonely death. Her surviving sons, Andrew and Rodney, distributed to the six Robertson grandchildren Ethel's $2,500 in savings, a few pieces of furniture, some china, and six copies of *Flame of Valor*, my grandfather's 378-page novel about a Belgian soldier in World War I. (To each copy was attached a handwritten note, from Ethel, that said, "This is the only copy of your grandfather's unpublished novel." I felt special when I received it. Then, one day I read it, declared it "abominable," and dumped it in the trash. In the 1990s, when I caught up with my cousin Judy, she mentioned the book and I said, "Oh, I can't bear to tell you, but I threw it away." She laughed and said, "You can have my copy.")

Ethel was an archivist. She saved every piece of paper, every photograph, every card that ever passed her way and she annotated every item with precise captions ("Outside John's tent at Camp Kearney, Nebraska. Johnny is napping inside. My hat was a Paris original.")

In 1990, I visited my uncle Andrew. He was a frail 75, not recovering from a recent heart attack. We sat in his den, left to ourselves by his third wife, a woman with whom he'd had a lengthy affair years earlier and who was palpably angry that now, only a year after he finally married her, he had lost his virility and was going to die.

"Faithfulness, marital fidelity, isn't a Robertson trait," he told me. "Not a good thing, nothing to be proud of. Maybe you have been more influenced by your mother."

He looked at me slyly. For once, I was influenced by my mother. I kept my mouth shut.

We talked about his brothers. There had been four of them, of which Andrew was the eldest. My father, Johnny, was born second, only a year after Andrew; a few years later came David, and, lastly, Rodney. Of the four, David never married. He never had the chance. After nineteen flights off an aircraft carrier in the South Pacific, he came home on leave with his crewmates. They flew out of Alameda Naval Air Station one morning on a training flight and crashed into San Francisco Bay. David's body was never recovered. At the Golden Gate National Cemetery in San Bruno, his marker is in the special circle for those lost at sea.

"The last time we four were together," Andy said, "was at a bowling alley in Berkeley in 1942. It was the night before I was sent to Camp Roberts for training. I had a daughter, Janet, and we made a pledge that whatever happened in this war, and after, we would take care of each other's wives and children."

"You didn't keep the promise," I said.

"I know. David, of course, didn't have children, and Rod and I thought Maxine had married a fine man. We didn't want to interfere. I'm sorry."

"That's okay," I said. "Everything turned out okay."

We talked about Ethel. After she died, Andy said, he and Rod cleaned out her apartment, stuffed the memorabilia into trunks and boxes, and stored it in Andy's attic. It was still there, he said, untouched. I was welcome to all of it.

"I can't look at any of it," he said. "Just the sight of her handwriting on a letter turns my stomach. Do you know that she wrote Thelma a letter"—Thelma was Andy's second wife—"and called her a vain woman, and this was when Thelma was dying! And Rod's wife, Alla, you know, she was terminally ill and she committed suicide in November, 1963, a few weeks before my parents' fiftieth wedding anniversary, and she left those three children. Ethel wrote the children a letter and said she didn't excuse what Alla did, and that the family was expected to attend the anniversary party, and 'be presentable'."

I hauled a carton of Ethel's detritus downstairs, and while Andy sat in his recliner wrapped in an afghan I unwrapped a small stack of letters tied with a pale pink ribbon that tore when I dislodged its knot.

The top envelope was postmarked Madison, Wisconsin, May, 1913, and it was addressed to Miss Ethel Gardner, First Pennsylvania State Normal School, Millersville. Carefully, I removed the letter, three thin sheets, written on both sides.

"My Beloved Girl," I read. "My visit was the most enjoyable one I ever took; I do not hope to take another with greater pleasure until our wedding trip. It was all so very beautiful and so very perfect…This trip has taught me more than anything else the real value of Her. It has drawn me more closely to you and has given your companionship a new meaning…Short as it was, it sufficed to lift the veil on new phases of your character and to give me renewed courage and faith in the ultimate goodness of God. He has abundantly blessed me in giving to me a sweetheart out of the choice circle of His Vestal Virgins."

In a second letter, written a few days later, the Vestal Virgin responded.

"…It is Sunday night, just about 'our hour' and it seems impossible to avoid the mockery of twinkling stars and the tantalizing call of the tree frogs from the sentinel oaks…One week ago today I rode contentedly by your side, watching the last sunbeams creep through the meshwork of the trees, sending long lacy shadows across the fragrant meadow and there was a song in my heart…"

I read on, aloud, letter after letter.

From the recliner, Andy chuckled, sighed, shook his head. And then I read:

"Dear Boy, my heart is full of the forbidden subject, and yet, we must acknowledge its preeminence in our lives if we are to have a future. For you, I sacrifice my sacred Irish heritage—save the theatrical brogue; surely I can revel in that minor talent to you alone—and my sacred Church, the beloved Sisters and Priests, the Blessed Sacraments, knowing that in His Wisdom He has joined our hearts and in His Mercy He will forgive."

There was a silence. I put the letter down and turned slowly to my left. My uncle was staring at nothing and his face was red and wet.

"Did you know this?" I said. "Did you know this about her?"

Andy shook his head. After a while he spoke.

"Until this moment I did not know that my mother was Irish."

He paused. "Until this moment I did not know that she was Catholic."

He hesitated and there was a change, a shift in his breathing, a gesture, I don't know, something that kept me silent and patient.

"Until this moment," he said, clinging to that phrase to anchor himself in an eddy of emotion, "until this moment I never knew my parents loved each other."

How do we untangle the filaments of faith, hidden and twisted over the generations, buffeted by doubt and fact? How unlikely is it that I would ever have learned why I am at peace in an empty Catholic sanctuary or would have known how the coloring books of Abraham drawing the knife on the bound Isaac would bring me in late maturity to repentance at Yom Kippur?

"Nana, hurry up! When you finish, we can play Apples-to-Apples!"

While I was making a mental list of all things blighted, dutiful for which I have to atone, my fellow inmates had finished the social studies practice test and the spelling words and had eaten steak quesadillas.

In college I somehow never learned Dante's nine circles of hell. And Dante never learned that he missed one, the one that forces a person to sit inside and write a column when outdoors the sunlight illuminates red and gold foliage and through the window grandsons can be seen running lay-ups under the hoop.

The official circles of hell are, in order from the gentlest to the horrific:

Treachery, lowest-of-the-low, has four sections. All sections are blocks of ice in which the fallen, the kings and queens of treachery, are frozen for eternity. The fourth section is named after Judas Iscariot, Dante's choice for the worst-person-in-the-world-ever.

As a counterbalance, virtuous pagans are in the first circle of Limbo in what is called "an inferior form of Heaven." How like life, I thought, where one rarely encounters the most interesting people at poolside.

That thought gave me a cosmic jolt. Whoops.

I checked the time. Only six hours of atonement left. I'd better get busy.

The list is long and I have miles to go before I sleep.

A BIT OF EARTH

Mary Ellen and I were taking a six-week course in Photoshop at Humboldt State University and this evening, as usual, we were barely on time.

My cell phone rang. I fumbled with keys, shut off the engine, and answered. It was John.

"A kid in Pennsylvania just called," he said. "He asked if you knew that your father's medal is for sale on eBay."

"That's a scam," I said, climbing out of the car and locking the door. I motioned to Mary Ellen to cross the street. "Everything's in the safe deposit at U.S. Bank. I'm late for class. I'll call you at break."

A beat, two beats. *Oh, Lord, it's the real one.*

At a break during class, I stepped outside and called "the kid," a 19-year-old pre-med student who collects military memorabilia.

"The seller doesn't know what he has," the kid said. "It's listed wrong and it's with a bunch of common medals. Dealers will spot it. The bid could go up to a thousand dollars. If it had kept its ribbon and pin it would have been worth up to five thousand. Especially since there's a story with it."

I asked how he found me.

"The seller has included a photo of the back of the medal. Your father's name is engraved there. I Googled it, and found all the stories about you, and the movie you made—*Letters Home*—and from the newspaper articles it didn't sound like you were someone who would have sold your father's medal. Or given it away."

The kid sent the link for the eBay listing. The Silver Star, battered and dulled, surrounded by a dozen or so lesser medals, was nearly unrecognizable in the flea-market lot. A second photo showed the flip side.

I enlarged the image. A rifle shot went through my heart.

Up to that point I had thought, well, amazing story, how unlikely, I already have a medal in storage, I don't have time to pursue the red-tape labyrinth of getting this back, it's just a symbol, a thing—with my father's name, belly-up and tossed in a box, a piece of junk jewelry, abandoned and dismissed.

I wrote the seller, who is known to me only by a user name—by eBay regulations, sellers are allowed anonymity regardless of whether or not they are unloading stolen property, unless a police officer produces a report. I explained the circumstances to the seller. I emphasized that in no way did I believe that he was the original thief. ("The people who stole our stuff probably only had possession for 10 minutes. The only things they collected were syringes," I wrote.)

The seller responded, asking for more information about me, to prove my right to the medal. I produced the proof. He responded, writing that he didn't know what to do, as there was already a bid on the item. (There is a simple procedure: eBay allows a seller to end an auction without giving cause, at any time before the auction closes.) The seller chose to stonewall; someone had probably clued him to the fact that he had missed a high-worth item.

Within a few days "box of medals, good stuff" sold for $611. The winner, from the looks of his history of eBay transactions, was a dealer.

I called eBay and spent most of a Sunday on hold. I was transferred and transferred. I repeated the story eight or nine times. By the time the evening ended I had had long conversations with representatives in both the Mediation and the Trust & Safety departments.

I was assured that Mediation would pursue the case, notifying both the seller and the buyer that eBay was aware there was prior notice that stolen property was being sold, and encouraging them to join a three-way email conversation (in which, unfairly, only my identity is known to the others). The ideal, said Joseph in Mediation, is for the three of us to "work out something." Joseph emphasized that by this, he, and by implication, eBay, did not mean that I was expected to buy the medal back.

The Trust & Safety department of eBay deals a heavier hand on stolen property issues, but that level of disciplinary action (lifetime exclusion from eBay, for starters) requires the involvement of a police officer and a copy of the police report.

Robert—I'd emailed him as soon as I learned about the medal, under the subject line, "This will blow your mind"—was discouraging about the chances of obtaining a police report for a car break-in in 1980. I hadn't been too optimistic myself. I seem to recall that there are warehouses somewhere in Brooklyn filled with pre-computerization paperwork from the NYPD.

I told Joseph in Mediation I was not going to let this incident pass.

"I always walk away," I said. "I've never sued anyone, I've never pressed charges, I've never taken a cent in a divorce. I've always decided that the hassle wasn't worth the bad karma. But this isn't my fight to abandon. Do you understand? This isn't about me. I'm not the one who died. Tell the buyer and the seller that. Tell them that I am not going to lose this medal twice. Tell them I will never rest until this symbol with his name is in possession of his family, of the people who look like him, who laugh like he laughed: his daughter, his grandson, his great-grandsons.

We will know him by his things."

All this I wrote in my column, "From the Back Pew," in the *Enterprise*.

A few days later Pete Giacomini sent me an email.

Pete was a little kid when I left Ferndale, a farm kid who went to Catholic school. I didn't know he existed. Now he lives in Wisconsin because being a little farm kid led to being a big national officer of Future Farmers of America, and those credentials don't lead back to Waddington Road, they lead to being a cheesehead and learning how to play hockey.

Like a lot of Ferndale ex-pats, Pete subscribes to the paper and stays involved with the goings-on. Over the years I've been a columnist we've become friends because Pete over-credits me with keeping his then-college-dropout son—the one who now speaks six or seven languages, has taught English around the world, has a graduate degree and is married—off the streets of San Francisco. That's another story.

In his email, Pete asked a few questions about the medal and the eBay transaction. I answered and he quickly responded. He'd done his homework. The seller, he had learned, was a woman about 30 years old who lived in New Jersey.

"What's your plan?" Pete asked.

I told him I'd tracked down the buyer from other transactions he'd made online, and persuaded him and I was the rightful owner of the medal. He was willing, I reported to Pete, to hold onto the Silver Star until he was reimbursed, either by me or the seller, for his $611 plus shipping.

It was spring. State and federal income taxes and county property taxes were due. At our house we were uncomfortably close to living off rhubarb and nettle soup.

"I'm sending installment payments until it's settled," I told Pete. "The buyer said that was acceptable."

Pete wasn't impressed.

"A lot can happen over time with something like this," he replied. "The longer you don't have it, the worse the chances are that it will be returned."

I didn't respond.

The next day Pete called.

"I'm going to tell you something," he said, "and when I'm through you're going to say, 'Thank you,' and hang up. There is nothing to discuss.

"Several of your friends," he continued, "have contributed the money to buy back the Silver Star."

Pete had located the buyer—a circumstance that concerned me somewhat because I had promised the man I would not release his name to anyone. According to Pete, the full payment was already on its way to a location in Florida.

I wanted to say more but I did as I was told.

"Thank you," I said and hung up.

Pete's plan went about ninety-seven-percent smoothly. The donated funds were received, the buyer packed up the medal, mailed it as an insured package, and sent Pete the tracking number.

The medal was delivered immediately. To someone in Quincy, Massachusetts. Pete panicked. I learned this part of the story later. There were a few "tense exchanges," Pete said, and the mistake turned out to be a switched tracking number.

A day or so later, I got a notice from the post office. I had received an insured package that required my signature. I went downtown and picked it up on May 19, a week before Memorial Day, five days before the sixty-ninth anniversary of Johnny's death.

Alone in the office, I unwrapped the scuffed brown star, dulled with grime. The star points extended to a half-dollar-sized diameter. Inset in the middle of the bronze star was the small star of silver. I turned the medal over and read the engraving: *1st Lt. John D. Robertson, Jr. USMCR.*

I held the star tightly, forcing the points into my palm. There was an ache under my sternum, a crying out and its echo. I'd felt it all my life.

My father had as many friends as a person can gather in a lifetime of 29 years. I learned this in 1990 when I read hundreds of the letters he had written before and during the war, and researched every name he mentioned. Pre-Google, this was an old-fashioned detective job.

In his letters from Marine training at Quantico through the years in combat to the end, he was with a friend he called Hedahl. They drank whiskey and played poker; they pulled practical jokes on a major they loathed (screeching a drunk version of "The Road to Mandalay" outside the officer's tent); they longed for home. No clues in dozens of reads, and then, a single reference, "…Hedahl, who was a high school teacher in North Dakota before the war, said…."

Was Hedahl alive? In 1990, World War II veterans were at least 73. And if he were alive, would he want to hear from me? What would I say?

I stalled on continuing the research, until I found myself alone in a hotel room in Washington, D.C. with hours to kill before I had to attend a meeting of a "Women in Business" task force to which I'd been appointed by the George H. W. Bush Administration. The position required showing up, being presented with the work of the staff, admiring it, voting for it, and eating expensive dinners.

In the privacy of a hotel room I had nothing more important to do than find Hedahl. Information gave me the telephone number of the North Dakota Teachers' Retirement Fund. I dialed.

"I'm looking for a man who taught in North Dakota, at least in the years before World War II," I said to the woman who answered the telephone.

"We aren't allowed to give out that kind of information," she said.

I was too close to give up.

"Please," I said. "This man was a Marine, the best friend of my father who was killed, and this may be the only chance I ever have to know what my father was like in those last years and days of his life. Please."

A pause.

"No one's here right now," the receptionist said. "They're all still out to lunch. Give me his name and I'll see what I can find."

"Hedahl is his last name," I said. "That's all I know."

I waited. My hands trembled.

"Are you still there? Good. His name is Everet Hedahl, and he must be alive because we're still sending him checks. He lives in Issaquah, Washington. Do you want his phone number?"

I didn't ask her for her name, and I wouldn't give it now even though she's likely either retired or the boss-of-all-bosses, but whoever you are, know that those fifteen minutes of your life profoundly changed the rest of mine.

A man with a rusty voice said hello, and I said, "I'm looking for Everet Hedahl who was a Marine in the war, and who was on Okinawa in May 1945," and he said, "You got him."

"Mr. Hedahl, my name is Wendy Crisp, and I have reason to believe—hundreds of letters—that you were a close friend of my father, Lt. John D. Robertson, Jr., Johnny, who was killed on Okinawa."

There was silence and then a deep choking.

"Oh, my God. Robbie," he said, and sobbed.

When Hedahl was able to speak again, he said, "Robbie was the best friend I ever had. I've missed him every day of my life."

I traveled to Issaquah later that year, and Everet and I got together several more times before he died.

I was sixteen months old when Johnny was killed. If there was grieving I have no memory of it. By the time my memories were fixed, no one was crying over Johnny anymore. My grandparents were stoic; my mother had remarried.

Everet Hedahl's weeping was the first time I'd heard anyone mourn my father. I hung up the telephone and slumped to the floor of the hotel room. My tears poured onto my face, my neck, my arms, my clothes. Forty-five years of not crying, released from the reservoir of sorrow.

Before I made the telephone call, I had showered and dressed for the meeting. I showered again, changed my clothes and went to the Senate Building to listen to reports on the progress of women entrepreneurs.

What did Hedahl say about Johnny nearly a half-century after he died? That he was smart and kind and funny, a loyal friend who laughed a lot. Except when he didn't.

"He was private," Hedahl said. "We were the closest of friends from Quantico through three years of combat in the South Pacific. Still, all I knew of his civilian life was that he had a wife and, later, a daughter. He was so careful with his feelings—a guy has to be when you're in a war—I didn't know his brother had been killed until another officer told me. You were the only thing he could talk about, and I think that was because he hadn't seen you. He talked about what he read in letters, what his parents and your mother told him about you. He was trying to make you real."

"Aren't you going to take that into the safe deposit box?" John asked when I came home with the medal.

"Not yet," I said.

I put it in an etched glass box that was a perfect fit.

"I'm not digging up your bones and burning them," I whispered. "You're home now.

"Welcome to my bit of earth."

ACKNOWLEDGMENTS

The first person to thank is Eunice Sanborn, who spent over a year reading columns and essays I'd written and sorting them into ones she liked and ones she didn't like. While I didn't always agree with her choices, it was a critical challenge to defend the salvages. Of course, there would not have been nearly eight-hundred-thousand words to choose from if Caroline Titus had not agreed to let me write a weekly column, "From the Back Pew," for her newspaper, the 138-year-old *Ferndale Enterprise*. And once that ball of yarn gets loose, where does it stop? There is my aunt and uncle, Hazel and George Waldner, who owned the *Enterprise* for 55 years, who employed me there from the age of nine, and who bequeathed me their ranch—in Ferndale, a place I would never have known had not my pregnant mother moved here "for the duration" of World War II, which for her, has lasted a lifetime. A big hug to my friend from childhood, Sue Laris, who not only has been a consistent presence in my life for nearly 65 years but who also gave generously of her time and her talents as an editor and publisher to read and re-read (and re-read) this manuscript while simultaneously hosting me at her home in Los Angeles. My daughter-in-law, Lauren Crisp, gets a big shout-out because she has been a vociferous, over-the-top supporter of my writing from the day our families joined. Her encouragement and enthusiasm have been a power-boost to me, as every mother-in-law will understand. There are people who have passed who gave me professional confidence and the rules of writing and living without which I could not have survived: Bob Forest, Bill Rolph, Zelma Rocha, Carl Sautter; and family members who, for better or worse, have kept me focused: Mother Pewsitter, The Ball, and my son, Max Crisp. Without Pete and Libby Giacomini, Caroline and Stu Titus, Sally and Steve Dolfini, Elsie and Don Giacomini, Jay and Gina Parrish, Irene Bryant, Milt Mossi, Kathleen and Dennis Leonardi, and Rosalie Paine and Scott Davis—there would have been no reunion with the Silver Star, no closure to a point of pain. Caroline Blattner did a yeoman's job of copyediting—twice—and all this would be nothing at all had not Wendy Madar founded a publishing house and decided I was worth the risk. And finally, I am able to write freely, to live freely, because when at last all I was looking for was "A strong, broad-shouldered man who loves to fish," I found John Lestina, a steady hand on a rough sea, and that has made all the difference.

WENDY CRISP LESTINA is the author of *When I Grow Up I Want To Be 60, Do As I Say Not As I Did, 100 Things I'm Not Going to Do Now That I'm Over 50*—all published by Penguin/Perigee –and *From the Back Pew*, as well as *Old Favorites from Ferndale Kitchens: The Museum Cookbook*. She has been a magazine editor (*Datamation, Savvy, Grand, Small Systems World, The Humboldt Historian, Our Story*), a newspaper columnist (Religious News Service, the *Enterprise*), a public speaker on women's issues, and a radio host (KEX Portland, Oregon). In the last decade, she has directed 14 historical documentary videos for the Ferndale Museum, including the award-winning *Letters Home*. Wendy has a B.A. in English from Whitman College in Washington and an LLD honorary doctorate from Middlebury College in Vermont, given in recognition of her writing and speaking on behalf of women and children. Wendy and John are Airbnb hosts on Waldner Farm, the ranch that is their bit of earth.